Time is Short!

The End of the World as We Know It

Strat Goodhue
Time is Short Ministries
Kaneohe, Hawai'i

Time is Short!
The End of the World as We Know It

Copyright © 2025 by Strat Goodhue

Time is Short Ministries:
Web- www.timeisshort.net
Email- timeisshortfreebook@gmail.com

Churches and other non-commercial interests may reproduce portions of this book without written permission, provided that the text does not exceed 1,000 words. When reproducing text from this book, please include the following credit line: "From *Time is Short!* by Strat Goodhue."

All rights reserved. No part of this book may be reproduced or transmitted in any form or by any means, for commercial purposes, without written permission from the author, except for the inclusion of brief quotations in a review.

Unless otherwise noted, Scripture quotations in this book are taken from the New King James Version of the Bible. Scriptures taken from the New King James Version®. Copyright ©1982 by Thomas Nelson, Inc. Used by permission.

Cover design by Strat Goodhue

Charts created by Mike Moreau – harvestmedia.com
Thank you, Mike!

ISBN: 978-0-9858418-7-4

Contents

INTRODUCTION: WHY READ THIS BOOK?   1

1- KNOWING THE FUTURE   5
    IT'S GOOD TO KNOW   6
    YOU REALLY CAN KNOW   7

2- DID JESUS PREDICT COVID-19?   11
    PESTILENCES- DEADLY INFECTIOUS DISEASES   12
    BLIND FAITH?   17

3- PROPHETS, PROFITS AND MORE PROPHETS   21
    PROPHETS   21
    PROFITS   22
    A TRUE PROPHET   23
    MORE PROPHETS   24
    THERE'S NO COMPARISON   25
    THE "PROPHET" JOSEPH SMITH   26
    THE "PROPHET" OF THE WATCHTOWER SOCIETY   27
    SO MANY WRONG PEOPLE   27
    JESUS VS. THE OTHER PROPHETS   28
    THE 100% ACCURACY TEST   30

4- PUTTING JESUS' PREDICTIONS TO THE TEST   33
    THE DESTRUCTION OF THE TEMPLE   34
    JUST A "LUCKY GUESS"?   36

5- TESTING, TESTING, 1,2,3...   39

    WARS AND RUMORS OF WARS   39
    FAMINES   41
    EARTHQUAKES   43
    SO WHAT?   46
    THE "THEY MADE IT UP AFTERWARDS" CONSPIRACY   46
    WERE THE SCRIPTURES CHANGED OVER TIME?   47
    WAS IT ALL A BUNCH OF COINCIDENCES?   49

6- HOW COULD HE KNOW?   51

    HITTING THE NAIL ON THE HEAD EVERY TIME   51
    WORLD-WIDE CHRISTIAN PERSECUTION   51
    THE LOVE OF MANY GROWING COLD   54
    THE GOSPEL PROPHECY   54
    SMART PEOPLE CAN BE VERY WRONG   55
    WHAT ARE THE CHANCES?   57
    THERE'S MORE, MUCH MORE   59

7- LOOKING BACK TO SEE FORWARD   61

    THE DAY PREDICTED 600 YEARS IN ADVANCE   61
    THE 1,900-YEAR LATER REGATHERING OF ISRAEL   63
    A LONG TIME TO BE AWAY FROM HOME   65
    JERUSALEM- "A HEAVY STONE" FOR THE NATIONS   65
    NOT JUST THE PEOPLE- THE PLACE   67
    NATIONS ALIGNING FOR AN INVASION OF ISRAEL   68
    WHAT ARE THE CHANCES?   71

8- AN AMAZING PROPHECY   73

    THE UNIVERSAL PRODUCT CODE   75
    THE SKEPTIC'S RESPONSE   77
    CONVENIENCE- A TOOL OF THE ANTICHRIST?   77

WHAT'S THE BIG DEAL ABOUT DIGITAL CURRENCY?	79
A BARCODE FOR BOWSER	80
A BARCODE FOR BOB?	81
THE BIG DEAL ABOUT DIGITAL IDENTIFICATION	82
"REAL ID" REQUIRED: "TAKE A NUMBER!"	83
WHAT IF PEOPLE HAVEN'T TAKEN A NUMBER?	84
BENEFITS ANYONE?	85
"TAKE A NUMBER!"	87

9- THE MOST AMAZING PROPHECY- SO WHAT?   89

THE PROPHECY	90
THE CRUCIFIXION	93
LIFELESS ON THE CROSS	95
THE THIRD DAY	96
ARE THE WITNESSES RELIABLE?	97
MULTIPLICATION, NOT SUBTRACTION	99
WHAT DO THE EXPERTS SAY?	100
SO WHAT?	102
THE BAD NEWS	103
THE GOOD NEWS	105
WHAT'S NEXT?	106

10- "THEY'RE GONE!" THE RAPTURE   107

THE RAPTURE- WHAT YOU NEED TO KNOW	107
WHAT IS THE RAPTURE?	109
IS "THE RAPTURE" MENTIONED IN THE BIBLE?	110
A ROSE BY ANY OTHER NAME	111
A PLACE LIKE NO OTHER	112
WHY WILL GOD RAPTURE BELIEVERS?	114
THE 7-YEAR TRIBULATION	116
THE TIMING OF THE RAPTURE	117

IN CASE YOU MISSED IT	120
WHAT HAPPENS NEXT?	120

11- THE NEW WORLD ORDER   121

NEW WORLD ORDER- GLOBAL GOVERNANCE	121
ORDER OUT OF CHAOS	123
RECOGNIZING THE ANTICHRIST	124
A MIRACULOUS HEALING!	126
THE "ABOMINATION OF DESOLATION"	126
THE PRICE FOR NOT FOLLOWING THE ANTICHRIST	127
THE PRICE FOR FOLLOWING THE ANTICHRIST	128
AN "IMAGE" THAT BREATHES AND TALKS?	129
WHO WOULD ALLOW THAT?!	130

12- THE END OF THE WORLD AS WE KNOW IT   133

THE LEADER OF THE NEW WORLD ORDER	133
A ONE-SIZE FITS MOST- GLOBAL RELIGION	134
WHO ARE THE TEN "KINGS"?	136
WORLD EMPIRES	137
WORLDWIDE DECEPTION	139
WHAT DECEPTION?	141
I'LL JUST WAIT UNTIL AFTER THE RAPTURE	143
YOU DON'T NEED A PREACHER	145
AFTER THE RAPTURE- THE 7-YEAR TRIBULATION	146
GLOBAL WARMING - CLIMATE CHANGE BY FIRE	147
THE TRIBULATION CHRISTIANS	149

13- THE END – THEN THE BEGINNING   151

ISRAEL AND THE ANTICHRIST	151
BEWARE OF THE GOG!	152
THE DESTRUCTION OF DAMASCUS	153
THE REBUILDING OF THE TEMPLE	154

DURING THE TRIBULATION   155
TWO WITNESSES   155
144,000 MORE WITNESSES   156
AND ANOTHER WITNESS- AN ANGEL   156
THE BATTLE OF ARMAGEDDON   157
TAKING CARE OF BUSINESS   158
WHO DO YOU SAY THAT I AM?   159
LIAR, LUNATIC OR LORD?   160
A VERY BIG PARTY IN HEAVEN   161
JUDGMENT FOR JESUS   163
JEWS FOR JESUS   163
SATAN CHAINED   164
1,000 YEARS OF PEACE   164
THE FINAL REBELLION   165
THE GREAT WHITE THRONE JUDGMENT   165
A NEW HEAVEN AND EARTH   166
THE ETERNAL STATE   167
THE NEW JERUSALEM   167

14- QUESTIONS PEOPLE ASK   **169**

DID JESUS REALLY EXIST?   169
HAS THE BIBLE CHANGED SINCE IT WAS WRITTEN?   170
HOW COULD A LOVING GOD ALLOW SUFFERING?   172
WHAT IF PEOPLE HAVE NEVER HEARD OF JESUS?   174
IS THE GOD OF THE BIBLE SEXIST?   176
DO CHRISTIANS HATE HOMOSEXUALS?   177
WHAT'S THE NEXT STEP AS A FOLLOWER OF JESUS?   178

APPENDIX 1: TEN PRE-TRIB RAPTURE PROOFS   **183**

CAN WE KNOW THE TIMING OF THE RAPTURE?   183

APPENDIX 2: QUESTIONS ABOUT THE RAPTURE 195
    Is the Rapture a "new" teaching?   195
    Are all Christians going to be raptured?   197
APPENDIX 3: BOOKS FOR FURTHER STUDY   199
    Other Books By Strat Goodhue   200

Introduction

"Truth will always be truth, whether or not people know it, understand it or believe it."

You may be reading this right now because a Christian gave you the book. Or maybe you are already a Christian and are curious as to what the future holds for planet earth. Since almost one out of every three verses in the Bible contains prophecy (predictions about the future),[1] it's good to have a basic understanding of what the Bible says about the future. Or maybe you picked up this book because an incredible event in history has occurred- an event that Bible believing Christians call "the rapture (the 'catching away') of the church," – an event in which hundreds of millions of "born-again" Christians will suddenly disappear off the face of the earth.

Really? The Rapture?

Maybe that event hasn't happened yet, and you are thinking this book already sounds like it was written by a lunatic. Don't put this book down. Many events in modern history would have sounded crazy to people of earlier generations.

Imagine for example, if you were born 1,000 years ago (in a day in which horseback was the fastest mode of transportation) and someone was to tell you that there would come a day in which hundreds of people would sit on seats in a metallic tube with wings and that this winged tube would fly through the air at more than 500 miles an hour- transporting hundreds of people at a time to distant cities.

---

[1] 27% of the verses in the Bible are prophecy- that's 8,352 verses!

If this person went on to tell you that indeed, not only would this flying tube transport people through the air, but there would be over 30 million flights of these winged metal tubes every year, carrying more than 4 billion passengers all around the world, what would you think?

And what if that person was to tell you that 1,000 years from back then, people would carry around devices that weighed about as much as a potato- devices on which you could have conversations with people thousands of miles away, and that you would be able to ask millions of different questions and the device would search for answers for you?

There have been many events in world history that would have sounded "crazy" before they happened, but once they occurred, they became what we now call "history," and we accept them as everyday reality.

The idea of hundreds of millions of people miraculously being lifted off the face of the earth by God and being taken to Heaven in an instant- may sound like insanity to you right now- especially if (like me in the past) you don't believe there is a God. But as you'll see in the pages of this book- there is undeniable evidence that God is real, that "the rapture" (the "catching away") will be a very real event in history and that it will happen soon. But don't take my word for it. Read this book. Examine the evidence for yourself. Because not only does this book lay out the evidence by which we can know there really is a God in Heaven and that the rapture will actually happen; this book also lays out other future events- events that will result in the world as we know it now- becoming radically different.

The End of the World as We Know It

In fact, it is not an exaggeration to say that soon-coming events will result in the end of the world as we know it. This book is written to prove that statement, but more importantly, it is written to prepare you for the future. And the preparations laid out in this book are not just the opinions or calculations of human beings; they are the instructions given by the One who truly knows the future of the earth- the One who created it. But again, at this point, you may think this sounds like crazy talk. Whether or not you believe there is a God who created the universe, I challenge you, if you are wise enough and brave enough to care about your future- read this book. As they say, "The proof is in the pudding." This book will do four things: 1- Prove that there is a God, 2- Prove that God wrote the Bible (using people) and the fact that the Bible precisely and 100% accurately predicts the future in advance- hundreds and hundreds of times (not being wrong even once)- proves that God wrote the Bible, 3- This book will tell you the future events that will occur around the world that will radically change life on earth, and 4- This book will tell you how to be prepared for what is coming.

Do You Want the Good News or the Bad News?

People sometimes ask each other, "Do you want the good news or the bad news first?" When it comes to the future of life on earth, there is both- amazingly great news and terrible news. There will be incredibly wonderful times ahead for everyone alive on the earth at that time, but before that wonderful and very long time period happens, there will be some difficult times, followed by a seven-year time period of what many would call "hell on earth"- the time of "trials" that the Bible describes as a seven-year "Tribulation."[2]

So, there is good news and bad news. And how you prepare for what's ahead will determine whether the good news or the bad news is in your future. That's why it is important for you to know the information that is in this

---

[2] Deut. 4:26-32; Isa. 13:6-13; 17:4-11; Jer. 30:4-11; Ezek. 20:33-38; Dan. 9:27; 12:1; Zech. 14:1-4; Matt. 24:9-31. This period is graphically portrayed in Revelation 6–18 (cf. "the great Tribulation," 7:14; and "the hour of His judgment," 14:7)

book- in fact, (and even though you may not believe it right now) it could literally have eternal consequences for you.

If you are already prepared for what is ahead, then this book can be an encouragement for you- so you can know about major world events that will be happening in the future and in what order, and this book can help you to be equipped to share with others- so they too can have the wonderful future that you will have.

But all of us should be in the same boat in terms of the future- we should all want to be prepared for it. Only a fool would rush ahead in the dark, not knowing or caring where they are heading. And as this book will lay out- you definitely can know what the future holds and how to prepare for it.

1

Knowing The Future

"Remember the former things of old, ... for I am God, and there is no other; I am God, and there is none like Me, declaring the end from the beginning, and from ancient times things that are not yet done."
- Isaiah 46:9-10

Have you ever been strongly convinced of something and then later found out you were completely wrong about your belief? I grew up in a non-Christian home. I was an atheist who made fun of Christians and their beliefs. I figured that some people created a myth called Christianity and some people who needed something to believe in- believed it. But I wasn't one of those people.

I remember as a child, sitting in the car as my mother drove to the airport for one reason or another. We would drive by a church in Honolulu that had a sign on top of the building that read, "Jesus Coming Soon." We used to make fun of the church, "I wonder if He's back yet." "No, I don't think that's His car out front." As the years passed, the sign on the church got rusty and they eventually replaced it with a new sign that read, "Jesus Coming Soon." I thought, "Too bad they didn't know how long it was going to take for Jesus to come back- they could have put up a more rust-resistant sign." At the time, I didn't know whether Jesus had ever even existed.

Fast forward to today- I am no longer laughing at an idea that I thought was ridiculous (or possibly crazy)- the idea that Jesus Christ came to the earth 2,000 years ago, then ascended into Heaven and that He is coming back to the earth again. I realize that some of you reading this may not even be convinced that Jesus was a real person- that He ever walked on this earth at all. If you wonder if Jesus really existed, you may want to read the answer to the question in Chapter 14- "Did Jesus really exist?" Then come back to this point in the book and read on.

It's Good to Know

Wouldn't it be great to know the future? If you knew someone who could tell you with 100% accuracy what will transpire on the earth in the years to come, wouldn't that be nice? Especially if the future is going to be great. You could walk through life with joy, knowing that great things are ahead. Like, if you knew you were going to win the Publishers Clearinghouse sweepstakes six months from now and would get $14,000 a week, every week for the rest of your life. Money certainly isn't everything but think of all the worry and stress you could be spared over the next few months as you encounter financial difficulties. You could just say, "I know this will be over soon and things are going to turn out great!" Webmd.com reports that 75 to 90% of all doctor's office visits are for stress-related ailments and complaints.[1] Some medical experts estimate that as much as 90% of diseases and illnesses are brought on by stress. Wouldn't it be great to not have to experience that stress?

And if you knew the future, think of all the smart decisions you could make. You could make sure that you would be in the right place at the right time to be in the best possible situation in the future. You could buy stock in companies that you know will explode in growth so you can be financially secure (and bless other people with your great wealth). If, for example, you were alive in 1986 and knowing the future, you bought 100 shares of Microsoft stock, which cost $21 apiece in 1986. Today you would have over $12M from that $2,100 investment (and almost $20M if you include the dividends earned over the years).

---

[1] www.webmd.com/balance/stress-management/effects-of-stress-on-your-body

And what if there are some serious dangers ahead of you? Dangers that could lead to great suffering in your life or in the lives of others. If those dangers could be avoided, wouldn't you like to know in advance what those dangers are and how to avoid them? Think of all the people that boarded the Titanic. The White Star Line, the shipping company that owned the Titanic claimed that "as far as it is possible," the Titanic was "designed to be unsinkable." People getting on the ship were excited, knowing that they were venturing out on a historic trip. The trip was historic, but not in the way the passengers thought it would be.

When the New York office of the White Star Line was informed that Titanic was in trouble, White Star Line Vice President P.A.S. Franklin announced, "We place absolute confidence in the Titanic. We believe the boat is unsinkable." Mr. Franklin's false belief didn't help anyone. Wouldn't it have been nice if people could have been warned ahead of time not to board the ship? Or even better- if they had advance warning, they could have alerted those in the wheelhouse of the ship and told them exactly where that iceberg was located and they could have made a change of course that would have saved more than 1,500 people's lives.

You might think, "Well, of course it would be nice, but nobody knows the future." If that's what you are thinking, as we will prove in the pages of this book, you are mistaken- and like Mr. Franklin, you are harboring a false belief. Some people already know many future events with 100% certainty, and you can know them, too. You don't think so? This book will prove it.

You Really Can Know

This book will tell you what the future holds- the great and wonderful things that can be yours in the very near future, and how to get them. And very importantly, this book will also clearly spell out how to avoid the terrible dangers that lie ahead for people who, like those 1,500 people who boarded the Titanic, made the tragic mistake of getting on a ship that looked like it was heading in the right direction, but was headed for disaster.

You may not believe in the supernatural. You may think it is impossible for anyone to predict the future- especially with 100% accuracy. If you are willing to examine some evidence, you will see abundant proof that demonstrates beyond any shadow of a doubt, that the Bible clearly and accurately tells us the future. And this evidence proves that we are living in what the Bible calls, "the last days."[2] You will also see that the most important events of the last days have already been clearly laid out for us. This evidence proves that time is short; that we are experiencing world events that are quickly leading to global changes that mankind has never experienced. And this evidence clearly shows that as incredible as it may sound, we are quickly approaching the end of the world as we know it.

Growing up, I used to see pictures of men standing on city street corners holding signs that read, "The End is Near." I used to laugh and think these people were crazy. While some of them may very well have had mental health issues, the rate at which Bible prophecy is being fulfilled no longer makes me think that a sign saying, "The End is Near" is an outlandish claim. What if we are getting close to "the end"?

What if God has clearly warned us about how to be prepared for the events of "the last days" so we can be ready, and so we can be sure that we are not on a ship that is heading in the wrong direction? Would you want to know about it, or would you rather be like an ostrich with its head in the sand?[3]

We, as people living in the 21st century, are at an amazing time in the course of human history. Many of the events that the Bible predicts will take place in "the last days" are taking place now- in our lifetime. Never before in history could a

---

[2] Acts 2:17
[3] This is simply an idiom. In reality, even ostriches do not hide their heads in the sand.

generation say that they have seen the fulfillment of these prophecies that the Bible says will take place immediately before the return of Jesus Christ to this earth. "Far-fetched," you say? Hold on. Let's look at the evidence for such a claim. Are we really living in the last days? Are we living in a time in which we could see the end of the world as we know it? Could that be true? Let's look at the evidence.

And before we go any further, I need to warn you. The future is not all butterflies and cotton-candy. There are some very rough spots in the road ahead. And in many ways, things are going to get worse before they get better. And the choices you make will determine whether your future is fantastic beyond your wildest dreams, or whether you will face trials and difficulties that you had never imagined could happen to you. If you want to hear that Santa Clause is real and that the Easter bunny is hopping your way, this book is not for you. But if you want to know the truth about the future, keep reading.

Do you want to know the future? Do you want to be able to make wise decisions that will benefit you and others greatly? Do you want to avoid the greatest dangers that you and all of humanity have ever faced?

2

Did Jesus Predict Covid-19?

> "It is hard to make predictions,
> especially about the future."
> - Yogi Berra

Almost everyone on earth is now familiar with the deadly, infectious disease we call Covid-19. In fact, it is reported that almost 671 million people have contracted Covid-19,[1] more than 7 million people have died from it,[2] and 13.64 billion COVID-19 vaccine doses have been administered worldwide.[3] Did Jesus predict Covid-19? You are probably thinking, "Of course not." And you are right in that Jesus did not specifically predict that a disease would come along that would be called "Covid-19." (And Jesus didn't predict any other diseases by name either.)

You may be surprised to learn however, that Jesus did clearly predict that in the times in which we live, there would be an increase in deadly, infectious diseases (like Covid-19)- "pestilences" as the Bible calls them.[4] In fact, as we'll look at shortly, Jesus predicted a dramatic increase in the number and severity of infectious diseases in the last days.[5]

Since the earth's population has increased from a few hundred million people at the time of Christ to more than 8 billion today, and with the increase in world travel (by airplanes, etc.) it is fairly easy to see why far more people have

---

[1] www.arcgis.com/apps/dashboards/8bce6fbdf96d458e801b09bf3416284c (Accessed- 5/19/25)
[2] www.worldometers.info/coronavirus/ (Accessed- 5/19/25)
[3] data.who.int/dashboards/covid19/vaccines (Accessed- 5/19/25)
[4] Matthew 24:7-8; Luke 21:11 (NKJV)
[5] Ibid.

been infected with deadly diseases in our day than at the time Jesus made the prediction (around 30 A.D.). In fact, by far, the greatest number of deaths from any disease in all of recorded history- 44 million people- was from HIV/AIDS which has only been around since 1960. And as of 2023, it was estimated that about 40 million people globally were living with HIV.[6]

Pestilences- Deadly Infectious Diseases

There have been historians since before the time of Christ who have recorded major events in the world, including pestilences. While we can't know the precise death toll of these deadly diseases, the occurrences of these diseases were recorded by historians of the day. Here is a list of the worst pestilences[7] since the time of Christ-

The first 1,000 years after Christ-
3 major diseases- Estimated- 24M+ Deaths
-Antonine Plague: AD 165-180 (est. over 5M deaths)
-Plague of Cyprian: AD 250-271 (300,000?)
-Plague of Justinian: AD 541-542 (Some estimates suggest that up to 10% of the world's population died. 19M?)

The next 800 years after Christ-
8 major diseases- Estimated- 54M+ Deaths
-The Black Death: 1346-1353 (Some estimates suggest that it wiped out over half of Europe's population. 39M?)
-Smallpox: 1520 Mexico (est. 8M deaths)
-Cocoliztli epidemic: 1545-1576 (est. 15M deaths)
-American Plagues: 16th century (A cluster of Eurasian diseases (including smallpox) brought to the Americas by European explorers. Some estimates suggest that 90% of indigenous people in the Western Hemisphere was killed.)
-Great Plague of London: 1665-1666 (est. 100,000 deaths)

---

[6] www.unaids.org/en/resources/fact-sheet
[7] www.livescience.com/worst-epidemics-and-pandemics-in-history.html

-Great Plague of Marseille: 1720-23 (possibly 100K deaths)
-Russian plague: 1770-1772 (possibly 100K deaths)
-Philadelphia yellow fever epidemic: 1793 (>5,000 deaths)

The last 135 years-
9 major diseases- Estimated 650M+ Deaths
-Flu pandemic: 1889-1890 (est. 1M deaths)
-American polio epidemic: 1916 (est. 6,000 deaths)
-Spanish Flu: 1918-1920 (est. 100M deaths)
-Asian Flu: 1957-1958 (1.1M+ deaths)
-Smallpox: 20th Century (est. 500M deaths)[8]
-H1N1 Swine Flu pandemic: 2009-2010 (est. 284,000 deaths[9])
-West African Ebola epidemic: 2014-2016 (est. 11,000+ deaths)
-AIDS pandemic: 1981-present day (an estimated 42.3 million deaths.[10])
-Covid-19- 2019-present day (est. 7M+ deaths as of February 2025.[11])

In summary-
First **1,000** years- **3** pestilences (estimated **24M+** deaths)
Next **800** years - **8** pestilences[12] (estimated **54M+** deaths)
Next **135** years- **9** pestilences (estimated **650M+** deaths)

---

[8] Henderson D (2009). Smallpox : the death of a disease. Prometheus Books. p. 12. ISBN 978-1-61592-230-7
[9] www.mayoclinic.org/diseases-conditions/swine-flu/symptoms-causes/syc-20378103#:~:text=The%20World%20Health%20Organization%20(WHO,WHO%20declared%20the%20pandemic%20over.
[10] www.who.int/teams/global-hiv-hepatitis-and-stis-programmes/hiv/strategic-information/hiv-data-and-statistics#:~:text=In%202023%2C%20630%20000%20%5B500,51.1%20million%5D%20lives%20so%20far.
  www.unaids.org/en/resources/fact-sheet
[11] www.worldometers.info/coronavirus
[12] This estimate groups all of the diseases brought by European explorers together.

14   Time is Short!

Here is a chart that shows the increases-

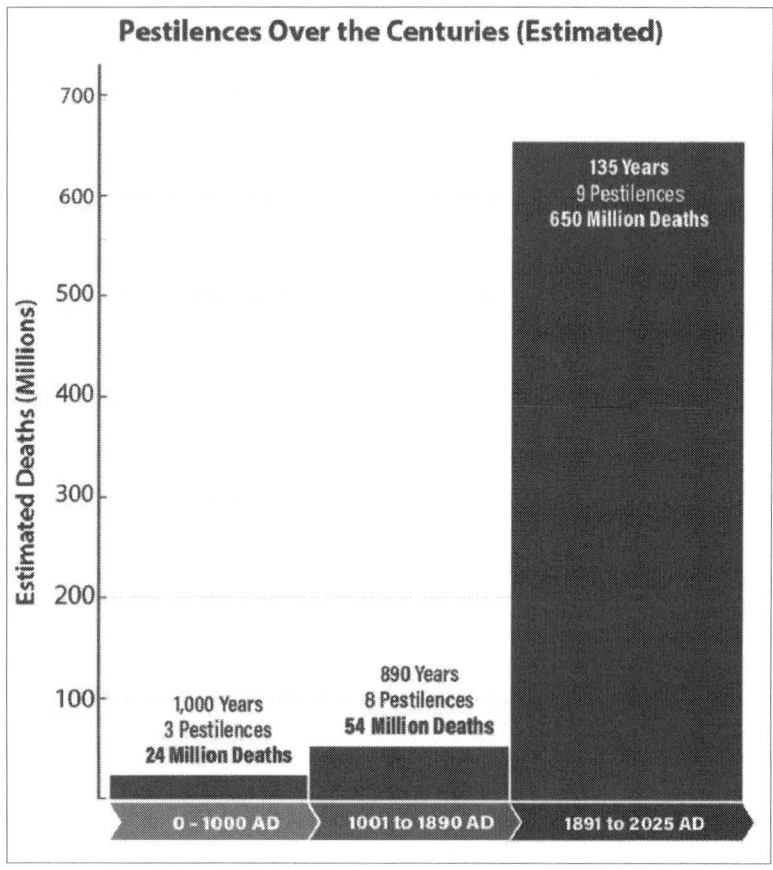

That means that there have been more than eight times as many deaths in the last 135 years from pestilences than there were in the all the previous 1800 years combined! And there's been almost as many pestilences in the last 135 years as there were in all 1,800 previous years combined as well. It's also noteworthy that four of the six deadliest pestilences in recorded history have occurred in the last 170 years or so.[13]

---

[13] en.wikipedia.org/wiki/List_of_epidemics_and_pandemics

Did Jesus Predict Covid-19?　15

So, according to historians, the number of pestilences has dramatically increased, and the number of people that have died from pestilences has dramatically increased as well- with the vast majority being in the last 100 years. Pestilences are dramatically intensifying in frequency and intensity- exactly like Jesus said they would be.

Of course, some skeptics who read this will say, "Well, surely the number of historians has increased over time, and they have gotten better at recording history." That's true. The ability to estimate fatalities has no doubt become more accurate over time, but do you think historians in the past wouldn't record the fact that hundreds of thousands or millions of people around them were dying from a disease? Historians have reported on world events since at least several hundred years before Christ.

Of course, we can't assume that the older fatality numbers are highly accurate, but unless the earlier historians were wildly inaccurate, there has definitely been a dramatic increase in the frequency and intensity of pestilences since the time of Jesus' prophecy.

At this point, the skeptic might say, "Well, the world population and travel have both increased dramatically over time. Of course, there will be more deaths and more outbreaks of diseases." Yes, the population has increased and so has world travel. But explaining the reasons does not take away from the accuracy of the prediction of Jesus. How could this small-town carpenter 2,000 years ago- know that there would be a dramatic increase in world population and travel? Was the dramatic increase of frequency and intensity of deadly, infectious diseases just a "lucky" guess by Jesus?

Some might think that with the tremendous advances in medicine since the time of Christ, that the numbers of deaths would be dramatically decreasing in our day, but they aren't. In fact, it's just the opposite. Just like Jesus said- pestilences are increasing like a woman's labor pains do, and they are increasing dramatically. And numerous health experts predict that things will most likely get worse- just like Jesus said they would.

Jesus was a carpenter[14] with no formal education, living in the small town of Nazareth- a town of only a few hundred people, located in Judea (now called Israel), a small part of the Roman empire- 2,000 years ago. How could this carpenter possibly have known that there would be vastly more people today that would be contracting deadly diseases than in His day? Was it just a lucky guess that infectious deadly diseases would increase dramatically over time? You might think so.

As we'll see as we look at a number of predictions made by Jesus, He did not just make a bunch of lucky guesses. No, it goes far beyond mere chance. What Jesus said 2,000 years ago about what would happen in the last days is perfectly accurate. How do we know that Jesus was referring to the times in which we live? We will look at that in a few minutes.

> The Bible contains 8,352 verses of prophecy- with 1,817 different prophecies- covering 737 different topics. Almost one-third of the verses in the Bible (27%) pertain to future predictions. And about half of those prophecies have already been fulfilled exactly as the Bible predicted they would be.

Someone might say, "Well, ok, maybe Jesus made one prediction that has come true." So, let's look at more of the prophecies of Jesus. Let's see if He really is "a true prophet of God." After all, Jesus' prediction of an increase in pestilences was not an isolated prophecy. He made a number of other end times prophecies at the same time.

But before we look at more of Jesus' prophecies, let's consider the predictions of the Bible as a whole.

After all, the story doesn't end with just a few prophecies made by Jesus. The Bible is loaded with very clear and specific prophecies that have come true. As a matter of fact, there are

---

[14] Mark 6:3. Note: The Greek word could also be translated as "craftsman."

8,352 Bible verses containing prophecies. And the Bible contains 1,817 different prophecies- predictions about the future- covering 737 different topics.[15] Almost one-third of the verses in the Bible (27%) pertain to predictions about the future. And about half of those prophecies have already been fulfilled exactly as the Bible predicted they would be. (We will look more at this claim shortly.)

Blind Faith?

This brings up a point that is worth considering. It is one of the things that makes Christianity different than every other religion in the world.

A lot of people think that believing in Jesus and the God of the Bible is like believing in Santa Clause, the Easter bunny, or the tooth fairy. They think believing the Bible is just a matter of blind faith and that while it may make people feel good, it really has no factual basis. They think it's no better than a good luck charm. In fact, even many Christians, when asked a question like, "How do you know the Bible is true and that Jesus is real?" will answer with something along the lines of, "Well, I just believe the Bible is true and that Jesus is real. It's a matter of faith."

As a child, I heard people say that after they died, they were going to come back in another life as an eagle or a dolphin or some other animal. That sounded good to me so I decided I would come back in my next life as a dolphin. I held on to that belief for a number of years. The problem with that is that it's like deciding you are a pineapple. You either are or you aren't a pineapple. (And I don't mean to be judgmental, but you aren't a pineapple.) You can't just decide one day that you are a pineapple any more than you can decide that you are your mother and father or that you are a platypus.

It's not just a matter of whether you believe something or not. It is a matter of truth. You may want to believe you will

---

[15] J. B. Payne, *Encyclopedia of Biblical Prophecy*, (Grand Rapids: Baker, 1980), 674-675

come back in another life as a dolphin, or that when you die, you will just cease existing, or that since you are a "good person" you will go to "Heaven," but simply believing something doesn't make it true. In order to find out if something is true, we need to examine the evidence. What evidence did I have that I would come back in another life as a dolphin? None. It was just something I believed that made me feel good. I had no evidence for my beliefs. How much evidence do you have for your beliefs about eternity?

Well, that's where the prophecies of the Bible come in. The prophets of the Bible (including Jesus) made almost 2,000 prophecies about the future and we can look at them; we can examine them in order to determine whether or not these "prophets" are reliable sources of information about the future.

There are numerous writings that claim to be from God. And we are not claiming that no other religion besides Biblical Christianity teaches any truth. The Bible stands completely alone however, in the degree of accuracy of its predictions about the future. In fact, the God of the Bible clearly says, "... for I am God, and there is no other; I am God, and there is none like Me, declaring the end from the beginning, and from ancient times things that are not yet done."[16] The claim is that nobody else can accurately and consistently predict the future like the God of the Bible. That is a claim that can be tested.

When someone or some religious book makes claims of truth, it is always important to consider the source. Is the source reliable? Is it accurate? Is it specific or does it make vague, non-specific claims like, "I see good things in your future." Unlike many psychics and prophets who claim to be reliable, the God who claims to have spoken to humanity through the Bible, makes a claim that we can put to the test.

---

[16] Isaiah 46:9-10

He[17] says, "... there is none like Me, declaring the end from the beginning, and from ancient times things that are not yet done."[18]

There are two very bold and specific claims in that passage of the Bible- 1) The God of the Bible claims to be able to accurately and consistently predict the distant future in advance, and 2) There is nobody else who can do that. And as we'll see in the next chapter, there is no comparison between the psychics, astrologers and modern soothsayers and the prophets of the Bible.

> **There are two very bold and specific claims in that passage of the Bible-**
> **1) The God of the Bible claims to be able to accurately and consistently predict the distant future in advance, and**
> **2) There is nobody else who can do that.**

---

[17] God is Spirit and is not male or female, but in the Bible God refers to Himself in the male gender. For more of an explanation, see Appendix question- "Is the God of the Bible sexist?"
[18] Isaiah 46:9-10

3

Prophets, Profits and More Prophets

"You can believe whatever you want to believe, but the truth is the truth, no matter how sweet a lie may taste."

You might think, "Well, for thousands of years, there have been psychics, astrologers and prophets who told the future. What makes Jesus and the Bible any different?" Accuracy. In fact, 100% accuracy. Do you know how many predictions the Bible has made that have been false? Zero. Let's look at some evidence. As we examine the evidence, you will see that the fulfilled prophecies of the Bible can not be explained away as mere "coincidences."

Prophets

Before I became a follower of Jesus, I was deep into the "New Age" movement. I had friends who were psychics and one in particular was very impressive in her abilities. People from a number of different countries would call her on the phone so she could "channel" information from the spirit world for them. (And she made quite a bit of money doing it.) She would sometimes describe situations and events that she had no way of knowing about on her own.

I'll give you an example of one of her "channeling" sessions. I was somewhat involved with a very small organization, a "hunger mission" that was working to help bring an end to world hunger. The hunger mission was losing their lease and would possibly need to relocate. My psychic friend knew nothing about this little organization. One afternoon, I mentioned the mission to her and asked her if the mission would need to relocate, and if so, where they would move to.

She sat cross-legged on a chair in my living room and put her fingers together like she was going to meditate and quieted herself so she could "channel" information from the spirit realm. She then told me that yes, the hunger mission would need to relocate, and they would move to a location that had a number of "small wooden buildings, like cabins" on the property. That's a fairly specific prediction.

A few days later, I found out that the leadership of the mission had been in dialogue with a local YWCA about possibly moving to their location. The YWCA had quite a few small wooden cabins on the property.

Was that an amazing fulfillment of my psychic friend's abilities to predict the future? Well, no. It wasn't. While the "spirits" she was in touch with were apparently able to see that there were discussions taking place between the hunger mission leadership and the YWCA regarding a property that had a number of wooden cabins on it, the "prediction" proved to be false. While the hunger mission did relocate (as she predicted) and the YWCA property did indeed have a number of small wooden buildings on it (as she described), the hunger mission didn't move to that location. So, her predictions were false, or at best- only partially true.

The "spirit guides" she was "channeling" were aware of events going on at the time, but failed miserably when it came to predicting the future.

Profits

A 2018 Pew research poll revealed that 41% of Americans believe in psychics.[1] But according to research into the reliability of psychic predictions, people's trust in psychics is poorly placed. There was a 12-year project to test the reliability of psychics' predictions called the Great Australian

---

[1] www.pewresearch.org/short-reads/2018/10/01/new-age-beliefs-common-among-both-religious-and-nonreligious-americans

Psychic Prediction Project (GAPPP). The researchers analyzed almost 4,000 published paranormal predictions made by over 200 people in Australia who claimed to have paranormal powers.

During the 12 years, there were 232 predictions made about natural disasters. The percentage of correct predictions involving natural disasters was only 5%. That's 1 out of 20. The overall rate of accuracy of all 4,000 predictions was less than 11% (and quite a few of the accurate predictions were "yes or no" type predictions, so they had a 50% chance of coming true by chance and quite a few of the predictions were quite vague).[2]

Does it make sense to seek out people to give you information about the future who get it wrong 90% - 95% of the time? And of course, when they give you the information, you will have no way of knowing which 90% of their predictions are false. A 90% failure rate is nothing to brag about (and a 90% failure rate would not get a 6th grader a very high grade on their math test), but while the rate of accuracy of psychics and soothsayers is dismal, their business is booming. According to one source, "psychic services" in the US raked in $2.3B in 2024.[3]

But even if these people do have "help from beyond," they are only right a mere fraction of the time. And no matter how vague a psychic's predictions are (being vague can make the predictions seem more accurate than they really are), you won't find a psychic anywhere who will claim that every single one of their predictions is 100% certain.

A True Prophet

The Bible, however, says that one of the tests of a true prophet is 100% accuracy. According to the Bible, "... if the thing does not happen or come to pass... the prophet has spoken it presumptuously [or "arrogantly"]; you shall not be

---
[2] www.youtube.com/live/dR3PtgRl-vM (Accessed- 5/20/25)
[3] www.ibisworld.com/united-states/industry/psychic-services/4413

afraid of him,"[4] (or "you shall not respect him"). That means that if someone claiming to be a psychic or a prophet makes a thousand predictions and even one of them is wrong, according to the Bible, they are a false prophet. Don't listen to them.

That is a very high standard- 100% accuracy. According to that standard, every psychic is a false prophet and you shouldn't respect their predictions- you shouldn't listen to any of them. Think about it, while psychics only get it right about one out of every ten times, even if psychics were right- half or even two thirds of the time, how can you know when they are telling you truth? You can't.

More Prophets

There have been many famous psychics and prophets over the centuries who have impressed millions of people with their abilities. Nostradamus, for example, was a man who lived in the 1560's, and yet people say he predicted a number of recent events, including the attack on the World Trade Center on 9/11. His prophecy that people believe predicts the 9/11 attack says, "Earthshaking fire from the center of the earth will cause tremors around the New City. Two great rocks will war for a long time, then Arethusa will redden a new river."

Believing this prediction is about 9/11 requires quite a bit of imagination. Did the attack involve fire from the center of the earth? No. Did it shake the earth? Not really. Did "fire from the middle of the earth cause tremors" around New York? No. Is "the new city" even an accurate description of New York City? New York is one of the oldest cities in North America and is not even known by the title "the new city." It does (like thousands of other cities across the globe) have the word "new" in its name (like New Jersey, New Haven, Newark, etc.). Did it result in "two great rocks" warring for a long time? No. Do "two great rocks warring for a long time"

---

[4] Deuteronomy 18:22

describe the two twin towers of the World Trade Center, or the US war with Iraq? No. Did the Greek deity Arethusa then redden a new river? Not that history records.

In another of Nostradamus' predictions, he predicted, "The great man will be struck down in the day by a thunderbolt, an evil deed foretold by the bearer of a petition." According to the prediction, "another falls at night time." This prophecy is believed by many to be a prediction of the assassination of President John and Robert Kennedy. After all, John Kennedy was killed in the daytime and Robert Kennedy was killed at night. The supposed "bearer of a petition" is believed by some to be the Astrologer Jeane Dixon and others think the "bearer of a petition" are those who had made death threats against Kennedy.

Of course, there have been many thousands of great men who have been killed throughout the centuries, and President Kennedy was killed by a bullet from a gun, not a thunderbolt. Guns were used in France 100 years before the prophecy was made. If Nostradamus meant to predict that "the great man" would be shot, why didn't he just say that? And if he meant to predict that the great man's brother would also be shot as well, why didn't he say that, rather than "another"? Why make such vague, non-descript predictions? And how was Jeane Dixon's prediction a "petition"? It wasn't. But as they say, many people believe what they want to believe, regardless of the facts. If people want to believe in the tooth fairy, they are free to do that. But it is a belief in utter nonsense.

There's No Comparison

Compare these false prophecies to one of the many specific Bible prophecies made about the coming Jewish Messiah. In a prophecy made more than a thousand years before Jesus was born, the Jewish King David wrote a psalm which accurately and specifically predicted events that would take place. One of the things David writes is, "They pierced

My hands and My feet."[5] When this prophecy was written, it must have sounded very strange to people, since crucifixion, the method of execution (which included piercing a person's hands and feet) used to kill Jesus, wasn't invented yet. In fact, crucifixion was not used by the Romans (who killed Jesus) for another 600 years after this prophecy was written. Have you known anyone or read a news report of anyone being killed by a process that included their hands and feet being pierced? Probably not. It must have sounded outlandish at the time the prophecy was made.

And it must have continued to sound outlandish to people for 600 years after the prophecy was made- until crucifixions started occurring. But it very precisely describes what happened to Jesus. The vague prophecies of Nostradamus and so many other false prophets cannot be compared to the precise detail and accuracy of Bible's prophecies.

The "Prophet" Joseph Smith

Joseph Smith, the founder of the "Church of Jesus Christ of Latter-Day Saints," was supposedly a prophet of God. Today, the organization claims there are 17 million Mormons ("Latter-day Saints") in the world who believe Joseph Smith was a true prophet, in spite of his false claims and prophecies such as his claim that people live on the moon- "The inhabitants of the moon are more of a uniform size than the inhabitants of the earth, being about six feet in height. They dress very much like the Quaker style... They live to be very old; coming generally, near a thousand years,"[6] or when in 1835, he predicted that Jesus would return in 1891.[7],[8]

---

[5] Psalm 22:16
[6] History of the Life of Oliver B. Huntington, 10, typed copy, University of Utah. See also: mrm.org/inhabitants-of-the-moon-truth-or-fiction
[7] History of the Church, Vol. 2, page 182
[8] For other false prophecies by Mr. Smith, see: mrm.org and mit.irr.org/failed-prophecies-of-joseph-smith

The "Prophet" of the Watchtower Society

Charles Taze Russell (the founder of the Watchtower Society of Jehovah's Witnesses) was supposedly yet another true prophet[9] but he made numerous false prophecies. He claimed that Jesus returned to the earth in 1874[10] but in 1889 started saying Jesus would return in 1914.[11],[12] Now, the Watchtower Society is again claiming that Jesus' return is in the future.[13] And yet today there are millions of people who follow the teachings of the Watchtower Society.

But it doesn't matter how many people believe or tell a lie. A lie by any other name is still- a lie. (For more information on the LDS church- check out mrm.org. For info on the Watchtower Society- check out: jwfacts.com.)

The Bible says it only takes one false prophecy to qualify someone as a false prophet- someone who shouldn't be listened to.

So Many Wrong People

But millions of people believe Joseph Smith was a true prophet. And millions of people believe Nostradamus was a true prophet. The list goes on and on. Millions of people believe that Muhammed, Charles Taze Russel, Edgar Cayce and Jeane Dixon, etc. were all true prophets. Since all of these "prophets" made predictions that didn't come true, they- according to the Bible- are all false prophets. It doesn't matter how many people believe they are true prophets. Again, believing you are a pineapple does not make you a pineapple.

---

[9] Watchtower 1917, June 1
[10] The Millennial Dawn, Charles Taze Russel, 1897 (Later renamed, Studies in the Scriptures, Vol. 4, Pg. 621) and Studies in the Scriptures, Vol. 7, p. 386 and Studies in the Scriptures, Vol. 7, pp. 68-71
[11] Charles Taze Russell, The Time is at Hand, p. 99
[12] www.jwfacts.com/watchtower/failed-1914-predictions.php
[13] www.jw.org/en/library/magazines/wp20131201/about-the-return-of-christ (Dec. 2013 Watchtower Magazine)

Millions of people for many years believed the earth was flat (in fact some people still believe that) but truth is not determined by popular opinion. It doesn't matter how many people believe they are pineapples. It doesn't matter how many people believe a lie is the truth- believing it won't make it true.

Jesus vs. the Other Prophets

So, what about Jesus and the Bible? Do they pass the 100% accuracy test? Since hundreds of millions of people can believe that false prophets are true prophets, could it be the same for hundreds of millions of Christians? Could they also be putting their trust in a false hope, just clinging to false beliefs because their beliefs make them happy or make them feel good or whatever? (Like my previous belief that I would come back in another life as a dolphin.)

Absolutely not. As we will clearly show in this book, the "sure hope"[14] the Bible talks about is not just a "blessed hope so." There is no comparison between false prophets and their writings, and Jesus and the other prophets of the Bible. There is undeniable proof that Jesus and the Bible are absolutely reliable in their predictions.

Neither the Quran, the Hindu Vedas, the Buddhist Sutras, the Book of Mormon, the Watchtower Society's "New World Translation of the Holy Scriptures," the writings of Confucius, Mao Tse-Tung, Nostradamus, nor any other book or writing compares with the Bible in regard to being able to validate itself of being of Divine origin. There is no other book, writing or prophet on earth (or buried in the earth) that compares to the Bible in its track record of telling the future in advance- with 100% accuracy.

As the God of the Bible says, "For I am God, and there is no other; I am God, and there is none like Me, declaring the

---

[14] Hebrews 6:19

end from the beginning, and from ancient times things that are not yet done."[15]

How do we know that "the one true God" made that statement? While there are countless soothsayers, psychics, astrologers, Tarot card readers and mystics who claim to be able to predict future events before they happen, the God of the Bible says, "... who can proclaim as I do? Then let him declare it and set it in order for Me."[16] As this book will prove- "Who can proclaim as He does?" Nobody. Only the God of the Bible can pass the test of 100% accuracy in predicting future events.

> As this book will prove- "Who can proclaim as He does?" Nobody. Only the God of the Bible can pass the test of 100% accuracy in predicting future events.

You might ask, "If there is a God, how could this God know the future?" The Bible tells us that the God of the Bible "inhabits eternity."[17] It makes sense that if there really is a God who created the universe and who "inhabits eternity," this God should be able to see all of time and know with absolute certainty what is going to happen in the future. It should be no problem for Him. (You may wonder why we refer to God as "Him." See Chapter 14- "Is the God of the Bible sexist?" for an explanation.)

So, if the Bible is what it claims to be- a book that is "God-breathed,"[18] then there shouldn't be any false prophecies in the Bible. Why not? Because if the Bible is true; God knows the future. He doesn't need to guess at anything or say, "Well, there is a strong likelihood that this or that will happen." No, there is none like Him- "declaring the end from the beginning."[19] And that is what we will prove in this book- that the God who created the universe and who knows "the end

---

[15] Isaiah 46:9-10
[16] Isaiah 44:7
[17] Isaiah 57:15
[18] 2nd Timothy 3:16
[19] Isaiah 46:10

from the beginning," superintended the human authors of the Bible so that, while using their own writing styles and personalities, they recorded exactly what God intended. The Bible was not dictated by God, but it was perfectly guided and entirely inspired by Him- it was "God breathed."[20] And the 100% accuracy of the Bible's prophecies proves that to be the case.

The 100% Accuracy Test

If, as the Bible claims, Jesus was a true prophet and the Bible is a book that has been given to us by the one true God, then we should be able to find lots and lots of evidence to support that claim, right? As a matter of fact, as I mentioned, there are about 1,000 Bible prophecies that have already been fulfilled. (Since many prophecies in the Bible are repeated, it is actually about 2,000 prophetic statements that have been fulfilled.[21]) And the majority of them are very specific.

Many of those prophecies were fulfilled long before we were born. For example, in just one chapter of the Bible (which was written over 500 years before Christ was born), the prophet Daniel, in just 35 verses (43 sentences)- made 135 prophecies that specifically describe the succession of different rulers of different empires and kingdoms.[22] And those 135 prophecies have been fulfilled so precisely that critics insist that the book of Daniel must have been written after the prophecies were fulfilled. But the evidence proves otherwise.

In fact, even if the critics' late (wrong) dating of the writing of the book of Daniel (about 150 years before Jesus was born) is accurate, some of the most amazing prophecies of the book of Daniel (such as the prediction of the exact day when Jesus would enter the city of Jerusalem in His

---

[20] 2 Timothy 3:16
[21] reasons.org/explore/publications/articles/fulfilled-prophecy-evidence-for-the-reliability-of-the-bible
[22] Daniel Chapter 11

"triumphal entry"- explained in Chapter 7)[23] were fulfilled hundreds of years <u>after</u> the critics believe the manuscripts of Daniel were written.

While the critics love to claim that the prophecies of Daniel and other prophets in the Bible were written after the fact, some of the Bible's prophecies that were written thousands of years ago are being fulfilled in our lifetime. Obviously, nobody can rightly claim that these prophecies (written in manuscripts that are thousands of years old) were written today. So, these are the prophecies that we will focus mostly on in this book- prophecies that have been fulfilled in the last 100 years or so, or are on the verge of being fulfilled. It is truly amazing that prophecies Jesus made almost 2,000 years ago are being fulfilled in our lifetime.

---

[23] The critics' late dating of the book of Daniel cannot possibly be accurate because the book of Daniel was already widely accepted as being Scripture hundreds of years before Christ, and Daniel 9:25-26 predicts the day Jesus would enter Jerusalem. This prediction will be explained in Chapter 7.

4

Putting Jesus' Predictions to the Test

"Test all things; hold fast what is good."
- 1 Thessalonians 5:21

Let's examine the claim that Jesus predicted an increase in pestilences (deadly, infectious diseases) in the time period the Bible calls, "the last days" and that these are in fact the times in which we now live.

It was a few days before Jesus was crucified. On the Mount of Olives, just outside of the old city of Jerusalem, Jesus gathered with His disciples (learners/followers) and spoke to them about the future and "the end of the age."[1] This message that has been called by at least one teacher of Bible prophecy, "the most important single passage of prophecy in all the Bible."[2]

For those who may not know much about the Bible- the Bible is made up of 66 different "books"- 39 "Old Testament" books (written hundreds of years before Jesus was born) and 27 "New Testament" books (written after Jesus was crucified). Three of the New Testament books give details of this prophecy by Jesus (the books of Matthew, Mark, and Luke).[3] These three accounts, written by different men, share mostly the same information but they each also share a few things not mentioned by the other writers. So, we will look at

---

[1] Matthew 24:3
[2] Dr. Tim LaHaye, Charting the End Times, Harvest House Publishers, 2001, pg. 34
[3] Matthew 24; Mark 13 and Luke 21

all three sources as we examine one of the most amazing and important messages about the future that Jesus ever spoke. (If you have doubts as to whether the Bible has been accurately passed down through the thousands of years since it was written, see the chapter 14 question in the back of this book- "Has the Bible changed since it was first written?".)

The Destruction of the Temple

Jesus' disciples commented on the beauty of the temple in Jerusalem. It was a magnificent structure that was 150 feet tall with white marble and gold that glistened in the sunlight. In response to the disciples' comments, Jesus prophecied about the future destruction of the temple and said, "Do you not see all these things? Assuredly, I say to you, not one stone shall be left here upon another, that shall not be thrown down."[4] This prediction must have amazed the disciples since many of the stones of the temple weighed several tons.[5] It would be a huge job to separate them and to throw them all down. What could happen that would result in that massive temple being dismantled- every single stone being taken off every other stone?

Well, forty years after Jesus made the prediction, in the year AD 70, this prophecy was fulfilled exactly as Jesus predicted. Numerous historians tell us about the Roman army's attack on the city of Jerusalem and the destruction of the Jewish temple. Many Jews fled into the temple to escape the wrath of the Roman soldiers and one of the soldiers reportedly threw a torch into a window of the temple and it lit the temple on fire.[6] As the gold of the temple melted in the heat of the fire, some of the gold seeped into the cracks between the stones.

---

[4] Matthew 24:2 (See also Luke 21:5)
[5] www.antiquities.org.il
[6] The temple was constructed primarily of stone, but also included flammable materials such as wood and cloth.

The Romans then took these massive stones off of one another in order to extract the gold that had melted into the cracks. The Romans' desire for the gold resulted in Jesus' prediction being fulfilled precisely as Jesus said it would be. Not one stone was left upon another. You can visit Jerusalem today (or go online[7]) and see the massive stones that were all thrown down.

> Jesus predicted the destruction of the temple- "not one stone shall be left here upon another, that shall not be thrown down." Did He just make a "lucky guess"?

When Jesus predicted the destruction of the temple, His disciples asked Him, "Tell us, when will these things be? And what will be the sign of Your coming and of the end of the age?"[8]

Jesus proceeded to give a number of prophecies about those two things- the destruction of the temple, and the events that would lead up to His return to the earth at "the end of the age." And as we'll see, the "end of the age" will in fact be the end of the world as we know it.[9]

This may sound far-fetched to you now but as we'll see later in this book, the Bible predicts that Jesus is going to return to the earth (His "second coming") and that He will reign on the earth as a King for 1,000 years. During the Millenium (1,000 year reign of Christ) there will be no wars, and the world will be a much, much better place to live than it is now- "Nation shall not lift up sword against nation, neither shall they learn war anymore. But everyone shall sit under his vine and under his fig tree, and no one shall make them afraid."[10] We will finally have the world peace that many people dream of having. (More on that later.)

---

[7] Search online for "stones as base of temple mount"
[8] Matthew 24:3
[9] The world will continue to exist but life on earth will be radically different.
[10] Micah 4:3-4

At this point, you might be saying, "Really? Jesus, a man who was crucified almost 2,000 years ago is coming back to the earth and it will lead to the end of the world as we know it?!" Yes, but again- don't just take my word for it. Let's look at some of the powerful evidence given to us by Jesus and other prophets of the Bible; evidence that will prove beyond any shadow of a doubt that the Bible is indeed- a book written (through men) by God[11] and that we can believe everything the Bible tells us about the future.

Just a "Lucky Guess"?

About 2,000 years ago, a carpenter[12] named Jesus lived in Israel, in the town of Nazareth- a town that had an estimated population of only a few hundred people. Jesus was with some of His followers ("disciples") and as they looked at the temple in Jerusalem, Jesus made some predictions. When you think about the fulfillment of these predictions, even an atheist or an extreme skeptic has to admit that the fulfillment of these prophecies is remarkable.

The first prediction Jesus made in response to the disciples' questions was not Jesus' most amazing prediction, but it is definitely remarkable. It was a warning against coming deception- a specific deception. "And Jesus answered and said to them: 'Take heed that no one deceives you. For many will come in My name, saying, 'I am the Christ," and will deceive many.'"[13] For all of human history, people have been lying to each other. But look at the specific lie that Jesus predicted- "... many will come in My name, saying, 'I am the Christ,' and will deceive many."

Jesus, a carpenter from a very small town in (what we know today as) Israel (a very small country in the middle east), predicted that many will come in His name and would deceive many people- and specifically, that they would claim

---

[11] 2 Timothy 3:16
[12] Mark 6:3. Note: The Greek word could also be translated as "craftsman."
[13] Matthew 24:4-5

to be "the Christ." The word "Christ" (which could be translated as "anointed one" or "Messiah") speaks of the long-awaited Jewish leader who would arise in Israel. Numerous Old Testament prophets spoke of this coming ruler who would be a deliverer for Israel.[14]

Since the time when this small-town carpenter from Judea (modern Israel), an area about the size of New Jersey, made this prediction, many, many people have come on the scene who have in fulfillment of Jesus' prophecy- claimed to be "the Christ." Even a quick search online shows dozens and dozens of people claiming to be Jesus, "the Christ," or "the Messiah." It's noteworthy that far more people have claimed to be Jesus (or the Messiah) than any other religious leader in recorded history.

> It's noteworthy that far more people have claimed to be Jesus than any other religious leader in recorded history. Did Jesus make another "lucky guess?"

Notice however, that Jesus didn't just say that many people would claim to be "the Christ" but that "many" people would be deceived by these false Christs. The "Reverend" Sun Myung Moon, just one of many people who claimed to be the Messiah, was believed to be the Christ by an estimated 3 million people.[15] Truly, just as Jesus predicted, many would come in His name, claiming to be "the Christ" and would "deceive many."

Did this carpenter just make an amazingly lucky guess? We certainly can't make a definite determination based on one prediction. Let's test enough of the prophecies of Jesus to be able to determine with certainty whether this small-town carpenter could possibly be a genuine prophet of "the true and living" God or whether he was just another charlatan in a long line of people who want to be famous.

---

[14] Examples: Isaiah 32:1; 61:1-3; Daniel 9:24-25
[15] According to Moon's Unification Church.

Speaking about what would happen before His second coming and the end of the age, Jesus said, "For nation will rise against nation, and kingdom against kingdom. And there will be famines, pestilences, and earthquakes in various places. All these are the beginning of sorrows."[16] At first glance, this may not seem like a very amazing set of predictions. But notice what Jesus said about the wars, the "famines, pestilences, and earthquakes in various places"- He said, "All these are the beginning of sorrows."

The ancient Greek word translated as "sorrows" in some of our English Bibles, is translated from a word[17] that literally means, "birth pangs" and some modern translations of our English Bibles read, "birth pains" or "labor pangs." Before a woman gives birth to a baby, she has birth pains. These pains start off as being less severe, then become significantly more frequent and intense. Let's examine Jesus' predictions. Has there been a dramatic increase in the frequency and intensity of wars, famines, pestilences, and earthquakes?

---

[16] Matthew 24:7-8
[17] The Old Testament was originally written in Hebrew, and the New Testament was written in Greek and Aramaic.

5

Testing, Testing, 1,2,3...

"In a time of deceit, telling the truth is a revolutionary act."
— George Orwell

If we want to know the truth about the future, we need to be willing to hear about the labor pains. If you are driving down a road at night and there is a bridge that has collapsed half a mile further down the road, you wouldn't be angry at someone who is standing on the edge of the road trying to save your life by waving their flashlight to warn you that you need to take a detour. You would be thankful for the warning- it could save your life. And according to Jesus and the other prophets in the Bible, there are events in the future of the world that we definitely need to be warned about. Are these prophets reliable sources of information?

Of course, a dramatic increase in pestilences is just one of the predictions that Jesus made about the last days. Let's look at a few more of His predictions.

Wars and Rumors of Wars

In answering the disciples' questions about the last days, in reference to the "labor pains," Jesus said, "For nation will rise against nation, and kingdom against kingdom. And there will be famines, pestilences, and earthquakes in various places."[1]

Let's look at the first prediction. Has there been an increase in the frequency and intensity of wars since the time Jesus spoke those words?[2] Absolutely. The following chart

---

[1] Matthew 24:7
[2] Matthew 24:7; Mark 13:7; Luke 21:10

shows the numbers of war deaths per century since the time of Christ.[3]

War Deaths Per Century

Estimated War Deaths by Century (100-2000)

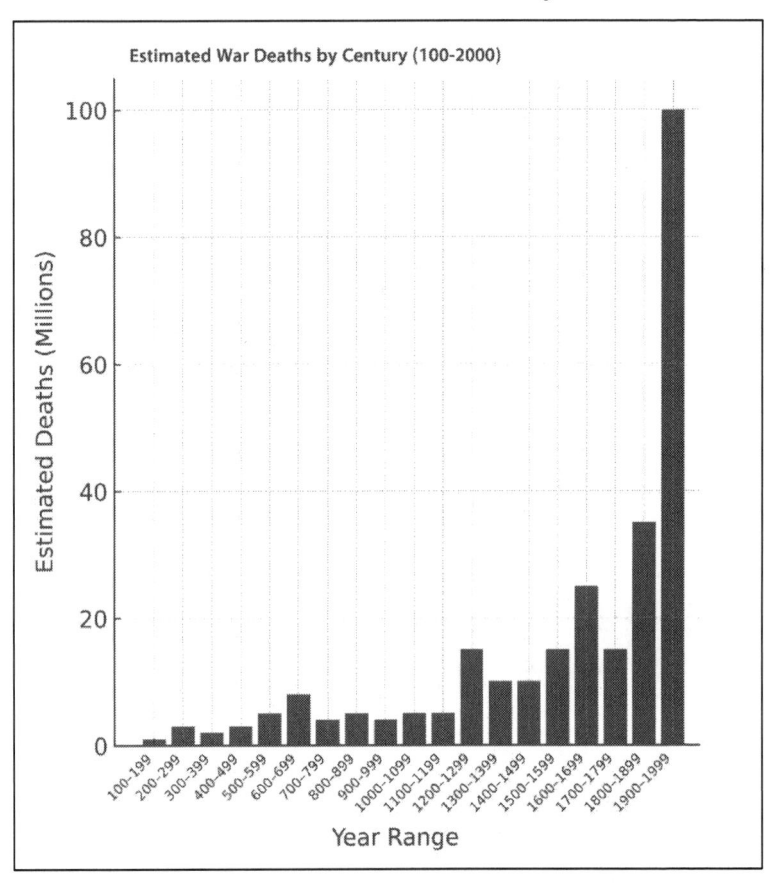

[Bar chart showing Estimated Deaths (Millions) on the y-axis (0 to 100) versus Year Range on the x-axis (100-199 through 1900-1999). Deaths remain low (under 10 million) from 100-1199, rise to about 15 million in 1200-1299, around 10 million in 1300-1499, 15 million in 1500-1699, 15 million in 1700-1799, 25 million in 1800-1899, and spike to approximately 100 million in 1900-1999.]

There has clearly been a dramatic increase in the number of people killed in wars since the time Jesus made the prediction in about AD 33. And just like with the dramatic increase in pestilences- the greatest increase in the frequency and intensity of the wars by far- has been in the past 100

---

[3] Matthew White, The Great Big Book of Horrible Things, (New York, W. W. Norton & Company, 2011)

years. Is it just a coincidence that Jesus prophesied of an increase in frequency and intensity of pestilences and wars, and that this is exactly what has happened? Did Jesus just make a couple of "lucky" guesses?

There have been about three times as many people killed in wars in the 20th century than were killed in all 19 previous centuries combined.[4] Jesus' prophecy is definitely being fulfilled.

> There have been about three times as many people killed in wars in the 20th century than in all 19 previous centuries combined.

Famines

Let's look at the next prophecy in the list of "last days" predictions that Jesus gave us. Jesus said, "For nation will rise against nation, and kingdom against kingdom. And there will be famines, pestilences, and earthquakes in various places."[5] Jesus said there would be a dramatic increase in famines. Has that been the case?

Famines have occurred throughout human history. The extreme lack of food has been caused by numerous different factors including war, inflation, political unrest, natural disasters including typhoons, drought or flooding, extreme cold, crop disease and insects such as locusts.

It is impossible to know exactly how many people have died in famines since the time of Christ, but from information gathered from various sources, there seems to be a significant change in the number and intensity of famines. Let's compare what history records about the first 1,000 years after Jesus was crucified, the next 800 years and the most recent 190 years. And keep in mind that historians have been serious about recording history since well before the time of Jesus.

---

[4] citeseerx.ist.psu.edu/viewdoc/download?doi=10.1.1.834.8051&rep=rep1&type=pdf
[5] Matthew 24:7

Famines Since Jesus' Prophecy-
The first **1,000** years- **19** famines (estimated **1M+** deaths)
The next **800** years- **132** famines (est. **100M+** deaths)
The next **190** years- **91** famines (est. **160M+** deaths)[6]

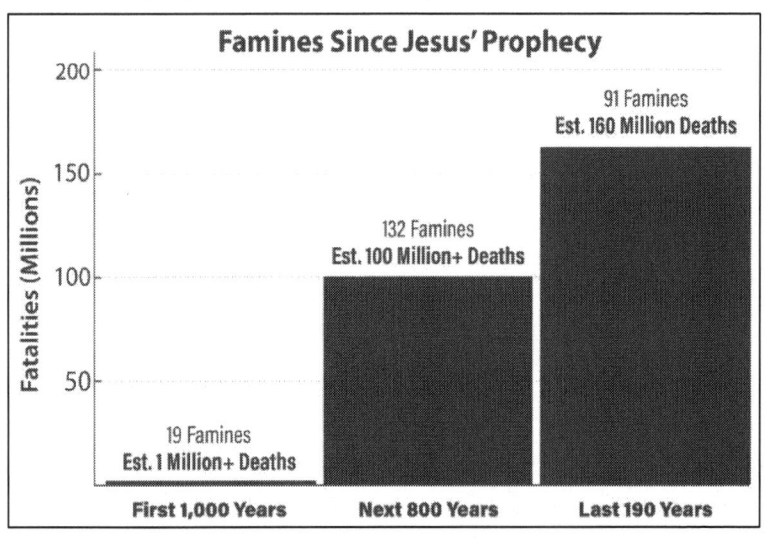

Famines Since Jesus' Prophecy

- First 1,000 Years: 19 Famines, Est. 1 Million+ Deaths
- Next 800 Years: 132 Famines, Est. 100 Million+ Deaths
- Last 190 Years: 91 Famines, Est. 160 Million Deaths

(Fatalities in Millions)

Fifty-five of those famines (with an estimated 87M deaths) happened in the last 100 years. It is remarkable that if the records of history are anywhere near accurate, the frequency and intensity of famines over the last 2,000 years have increased dramatically, with fatalities increasing from about 1,000 people per year to about 842,000 people per year. That's an 84,000% increase!

To be fair, we have to admit that even though there were historians recording information about famines that occurred in the 2,000 years since Christ, there are no accurate numbers available to us today of the number of fatalities for famines that occurred in the first 1,000 years or more after Christ. But again, if there were hundreds of thousands or millions of people dying in these famines, surely, historians would have

---

[6] en.wikipedia.org/wiki/List_of_famines (accessed 10/5/20), listverse.com/2013/04/10/10-terrible-famines-in-history (accessed 10/5/20)

given us some indication of that. There has clearly been an increase in both the number of famines and the intensity (number of fatalities) of those famines over the last 2,000 years.

According to worldatlas.com, the worst famine in history took place not in the year AD 50, 500 or 1500, but in China between 1959 and 1961, with estimated deaths ranging from 20 to 50 million.[7] And while the estimated numbers of people killed by famines varies between sources, it is estimated that between the 1860's and 2016, a total of 128 million people died in famines.[8] It's noteworthy that these massive numbers of fatalities happened not in the first 1900 years after Christ, but in the most recent 170 years or so.

In addition to recent famine fatalities, according to the 2024 Global Report on Food Crises,[9] in 2023, there were 282 million people in 59 countries who experienced high levels of acute food insecurity requiring urgent food and livelihood assistance.[10] That's an increase of almost 170 million people from about 113 million people just five years earlier.

It seems quite clear that just as Jesus predicted, we have seen a dramatic increase in the frequency and intensity of famines around the world- especially in more recent years.

Earthquakes

In His prophecy of the last days, Jesus also said, "there will be great earthquakes in various places."[11] The Greek word translated in our English Bibles as "great" is the word "megas" - the word we get our English word "mega" from. Jesus was not just predicting earthquakes. He was predicting "mega"

---

[7] www.worldatlas.com/articles/the-deadliest-famines-ever.html
[8] ourworldindata.org/famines
[9] www.fsinplatform.org/report/global-report-food-crises-2024/#acute-food-insecurity
[10] Ibid.
[11] Luke 21:11, Mark 13:8

earthquakes- massive earthquakes in numerous ("various") places.[12]

If Jesus' prophecy was correct, we should be seeing a dramatic increase in the frequency and intensity in the "birth pains" of earthquakes. Is that in fact what we see? We don't have records of the magnitude of ancient earthquakes since people did not have a way to measure the magnitude of earthquakes until late in the 19th century. Historians through the ages could describe the effects of earthquakes, but the descriptions would just be estimates of how large the earthquakes actually were. And if they occurred far away from populated areas, we have no way of knowing that they even happened.

But times and technology have changed. Starting in the early 20th century when the seismograph was invented, people started monitoring earthquakes around the world.[13,14]

Through the years, a lot of people started pointing to the increase in the number of earthquakes as a sign that Jesus' return is near. At one point, the USGS (United States Geological Survey) put out a letter stating that there hasn't been an increase in the number of earthquakes in recent times. But more recently, the USGS has been forced by the facts to change their position.

> At one point, the USGS put out a letter stating that there hasn't been an increase in the number of earthquakes in recent times. But more recently, the USGS has been forced by the facts to change their position.

I thought I would look for myself, since you read all kinds of things on the web and hear all kinds of things from the corporate controlled media. I went to the USGS website and did some searching. And guess what I found regarding "Significant Earthquakes"? According to USGS, in 1960, there

---

[12] Mark 13:8
[13] igppweb.ucsd.edu/~agnew/Pubs/agnew.a66.pdf
[14] en.wikipedia.org/wiki/Seismology

were 64 "significant" earthquakes. In 1990, there were 85 significant earthquakes. In 2019, there were 152. Did I just "cherry pick" these figures to show an increase? No.

According to the USGS, in 1900 a global network of 40 seismic stations was operational[15] and seismographs were in wide use around the world by the 1920's.

Per the USGS- "According to long-term records (since about 1900)... The year with the largest total was 2010, with 24 major earthquakes (greater than or equal to magnitude 7.0).... the annual long-term average of 16 major earthquakes."[16]

You can look up the data and see for yourself if you'd like- https://earthquake.usgs.gov/earthquakes/search.

Again, per the USGS- "In the past 44 years, from 1973 through 2017, our records show that we have exceeded the long-term average number of major earthquakes only 11 times, in 1976, 1990, 1995, 1999, 2007, 2009, 2010, 2011, 2013, 2015, and 2016." [17] Am I the only one that notices that the increase in the average number of major earthquakes has occurred recently- and not back in the 1970's or 1980's?

In fact, according to those USGS figures, the number of years in which the number of major earthquakes has exceeded the average has almost doubled in the last 30 years compared to the previous 30 years.

---

[15] earthquake.usgs.gov/education/eqscience-timeline.php
[16] www.usgs.gov/faqs/why-are-we-having-so-many-earthquakes-has-naturally-occurring-earthquake-activity-been?qt-news_science_products=0#qt-news_science_products (accessed 08-31-25)
[17] www.indiatvnews.com/fyi/rising-number-of-earthquake-2020-meaning-is-a-big-earthquake-eminent-experts-629831

Here's a chart that shows the increase in the frequency of large earthquakes since 1900-

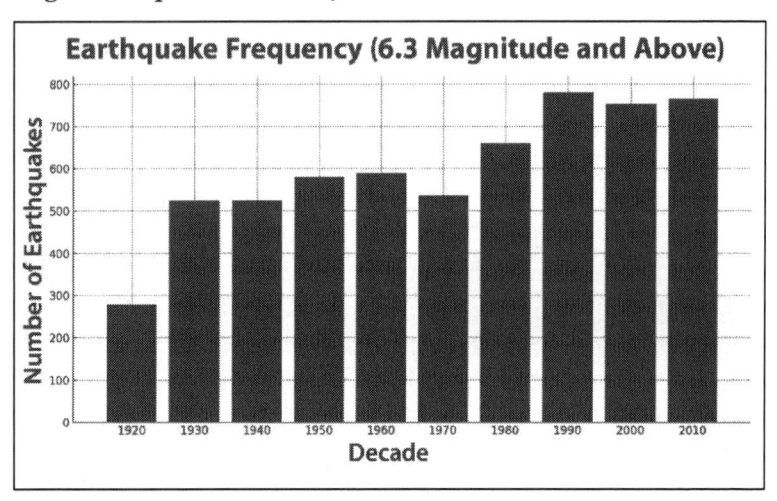

Earthquake Frequency (6.3 Magnitude and Above)

[Bar chart showing Number of Earthquakes by Decade from 1920 to 2010, with values rising from about 280 in 1920 to around 750-780 in 1990-2010]

So What?

Ok, let's consider what we have seen so far. Is it really all that impressive? About 2,000 years ago, there was a carpenter[18] named Jesus who lived in a town of a few hundred people in Israel. He was with some of His followers and as they looked at the temple in Jerusalem, He made some predictions about the "end of the age."[19] When you think about the fulfillment of these predictions, even an atheist or an extreme skeptic has to admit that the fulfillment of these prophecies is remarkable.

The "They made it all up after the fact" Conspiracy

Before we look at the likelihood of the prophecies of Jesus all being fulfilled by chance, it might be good to address a concern you might have at this point. How do we know that Jesus even made those predictions? After all, couldn't someone have made up stories about Jesus and then written

---

[18] Mark 6:3. Note: The Greek word could also be translated as "craftsman."
[19] Matthew 24:3

them down after the fact in order to trick people? Couldn't someone have observed the destruction of the temple in AD 70 and then in AD 75 or 90 made up a story that Jesus had predicted the temple being destroyed? Then, they could brag and say, "Hey! Look at all these fulfilled prophecies!" Nope. That's not what happened. How do we know?

First of all, the destruction of the Jewish temple in Jerusalem in AD 70 by the Roman army under the command of the General Titus is a well-documented fact of history.

At the time of the destruction of the temple, a large part of the Jewish population was either massacred or fled to other countries. Needless to say, many Jewish Christians (who had read or heard of Jesus' warning about the coming destruction of the temple) took their Scriptures with them when they fled and went into exile. And the vast majority of these Christians never returned to the land of Israel.

Were the Scriptures Changed Over Time?

Many Jews fled to Mesopotamia (modern day Iraq), and the rest fled to lands around the Mediterranean, including (countries now known as) Spain, France, Italy, Greece, Cyprus, and Turkey. They settled in these countries and now, almost 2,000 years later, ancient manuscripts (some now translated into different languages) from these different countries have been found and compared to one another. And remarkably, they are practically identical to each other.

What this tells us is that all of these different manuscripts have a common origin- Judea (modern day Israel). And these discoveries don't just tell us where the original manuscripts came from, but also- when. Since the Jews were scattered into all these countries in AD 70, we know that the original sources of these many manuscripts were written before AD 70.

The "New Testament" manuscripts (written after Jesus died in about AD 33) have a noteworthy history. The ancient manuscript evidence is very impressive, with 24,000 known copies, more than 5,000 of which are complete (they include the entire New Testament). Some date as early as the second and third centuries AD with some ancient manuscripts being discovered as recently as 2023.[20] That's an almost 2,000-year track record of discoveries of ancient manuscripts that are almost identical.

What this tells us is that the New Testament hasn't changed from when it was first written. (For more support for this claim, I highly recommend the books, *Evidence that Demands a Verdict*, by Josh McDowell, and *A General Introduction to the Bible*, by Norman Geisler and William Nix.)[21]

So, let's get back to the question of whether the fulfillment of the predictions of Jesus was amazing or just coincidence.

First, Jesus predicted that the massive temple in Jerusalem would be destroyed. And He said specifically that, "not one stone shall be left here upon another, that shall not be thrown down."[22] Forty years later, in spite of the fact that some of the stones weighed several tons, Jesus' prophecy was fulfilled exactly as Jesus said it would be. Every stone of the temple was thrown down and 2,000 years later, there they still sit- all in a heap.

---

[20] phys.org/news/2023-04-fragment-year-old-testament.html
[21] We will examine the reliability of the Old Testament later on in this book.
[22] Matthew 24:2

Was it all a Bunch of Coincidences?

Was it a fluke that Jesus was able to predict the destruction of the temple so precisely- not only predicting what would happen but the manner in which it would happen- "not one stone left upon another"? You might think it was a "lucky" guess, so let's keep going.

Next, Jesus told His followers that many would come on the scene claiming to be the Messiah and would deceive many. Well, what do you know, this small-town carpenter hit the nail on the head (so to speak) again. Two-thousand years ago this carpenter predicted that in time, "many" deceivers would come along claiming to be "the Christ" and that "many" people would be deceived into believing these charlatans. What do you know, just as Jesus predicted- many have come along, claiming to be the Christ and have deceived many (even millions of) people.

Next, Jesus told His followers that there would be a series of noteworthy events leading up to "the end of the age" that would increase like labor pains. Specifically, Jesus predicted that these events would include wars, famines, pestilences and earthquakes.

What has happened since Jesus made those predictions? As we have seen- there has been a dramatic increase in intensity and frequency of wars, a dramatic increase in intensity and frequency of famines, a dramatic increase in intensity and frequency of pestilences and a dramatic increase in intensity and frequency of earthquakes (at least in the last 100 years or so)- every one of the events that Jesus predicted would see a dramatic increase (although we can't know for sure as far as the possible long-term increase in earthquakes). And just like with labor pains, the increase has been exponential- especially in the last 100 years or so. And the recent increases have been dramatic in the case of every one of those predictions.[23]

If those were the only prophecies of Jesus that had been fulfilled exactly as they were predicted, maybe we could write them off as just being a series of "very, very, very lucky guesses." How could a carpenter from a tiny little town in Israel- 2,000 years ago, perfectly foretell the future in regard to all of these events? Some would say it's possibly just a bunch of coincidences.

But those events are just the tip of the iceberg when it comes to the amazing prophecies of Jesus that have been fulfilled exactly as He said they would be. As we'll see in the next chapter, there is absolutely no way that the very specific prophecies of the Bible could be fulfilled by chance. There is much more going on here than just a bunch of "lucky guesses" or "coincidences."

---

[23] Admittedly, we aren't able to determine the long-term trend for earthquakes.

6

How Could He Know?

"Facts are stubborn things; and whatever may be our wishes, our inclinations, or the dictates of our passions, they cannot alter the state of facts and evidence."
- John Adams, 2nd US President

The Carpenter Hit the Nail on the Head Every Time

So far, we have a list of eight specific predictions of Jesus:
1- The destruction of the temple in Jerusalem
2- Not one stone left on another
3- Many false Christs
4- Many people deceived by the false Christs

A dramatic increase in frequency & intensity over time of-
5- Wars
6- Famines
7- Pestilences
8- Earthquakes

World-wide Christian Persecution

After making these very specific predictions, Jesus said to His followers, "Then they will deliver you up to tribulation and kill you, and you will be hated by all nations for My name's sake."[1] There are two things that are predicted in this prophecy. One is that Jesus' followers would be persecuted and even killed because they were followers of Jesus. The second one is that the persecution would be global- that people all over the world would hate and persecute Jesus' followers.

---

[1] Matthew 24:9

These predictions were made 2,000 years ago. It's estimated that more than 70 million Christians have been martyred over the last 2,000 years, more than half of which died in the 20th century under fascist and communist regimes. It's also estimated that 1 million Christians were killed between 2001 and 2010 and about 900,000 were killed from 2011 to 2020.[2]

It is estimated that more Christians have been martyred (killed because they were Christians) in the 20th century than in all 19 previous centuries combined.

People in nations around the world have persecuted and even killed the followers of a number of religions. Pew Research Center reports that, "Harassment of religious groups continues to be reported in more than 90% of countries."[3] But guess which religion is at the top of the list? You guessed it- Christianity. According to Pew research, Christians are "harassed" in 145 different countries. Pew defines "harassed" as mistreatment ranging "from verbal abuse to physical violence and killings."

More than 14,000 churches, Christian schools, hospitals and other buildings were attacked or closed in 2024, including an estimated 10,000 churches in China that were closed and 2,228 churches in India that were attacked.[4]

At first glance, Jesus' prediction of a worldwide following, persecution and martyrdom might not seem like a very impressive prediction. But think about this one for a minute- what is the likelihood that a very small-town carpenter in the middle east, living in the first century would accurately predict that people from all over the world would persecute and even kill his followers?

Could it be that this small-town carpenter in the middle east just had a massive ego and imagined He would have a

---

[2] www.gordonconwell.edu/blog/christian-martyrdom-who-why-how

[3] www.pewresearch.org/religion/2020/11/10/harassment-of-religious-groups-continues-to-be-reported-in-more-than-90-of-countries

[4] www.opendoorsus.org/en-US/persecution/countries

worldwide following? And furthermore, that there would be worldwide and even deadly persecution of His followers? Has anyone else in recorded history made such a prediction and had it come true? Did the small-town carpenter who made all those other fulfilled prophecies just happen to make another amazingly "lucky guess"? Or could it be that He was not arrogant at all, that it was not a "lucky guess," but that He was a true prophet- speaking one more prophecy 2,000 years ago that we see being fulfilled dramatically- even in our lifetime?

What do you know- this 1st century small town carpenter in the middle east hit the nail on the head again! He was definitely a lot more than a carpenter.

But Jesus wasn't finished prophesying. In the next sentence, Jesus said, "And then many will be offended, will betray one another, and will hate one another."[5] Sure enough, parents betray their Christian children, friends and brothers and sisters betray Christians all over the world and hand them over to persecutors. Just as Jesus predicted about the end times, "... brother will betray brother to death, and a father his child; and children will rise up against parents and cause them to be put to death. And you will be hated by all for My name's sake."[6]

The next prediction of Jesus that Matthew mentions after the persecution of the followers of Jesus was, "Then many false prophets will rise up and deceive many."[7] We don't need to look at many examples to realize that here again, the Carpenter hit the nail on the head. There is no comparison between the every-time accurate predictions of Jesus and the dismal track record of modern psychics (with their 1 out of 20 predictions being accurate) and other false prophets such as Mormonism's Joseph Smith or the Watchtower Society's Charles Taze Russell.

---

[5] Matthew 24:10
[6] Mark 13:12. The Greek word translated as "all" in the New Testament does not necessarily mean "every single one." It is a general term.
[7] Matthew 24:11

The Love of Many Growing Cold

After speaking of the many false prophets who would arise, Jesus said, "And because lawlessness will abound, the love of many will grow cold." These are very difficult predictions to put to the test- especially over the last 2,000 years. How could we accurately measure "lawlessness" and "love"? While many would argue that society seems to be growing more lawless (i.e.- unrighteous) and less loving (more indifferent) in our lifetime ("Things just aren't what they used to be,") this would be a matter of opinion. So, we won't spend much time on this one.

Research led by a University of Georgia sociologist on the growth in the scope and scale of felony convictions found that, as of 2010, people with felony convictions accounted for 8 percent of the overall US population. That means that almost one out of every ten people in the US are convicted felons.[8] This is alarming but again, this is not proof that "lawlessness" (or unrighteousness) has increased since the time of Christ. We simply have no way to accurately measure the trend of people's "love" or "lawlessness" over the last 2,000 years, so (while Jesus' prophecy may very well be fulfilled) we will not claim that those prophecies of Jesus were definitely fulfilled.

> As of 2010, people with felony convictions accounted for 8% of the overall US population. That means that almost one out of every ten people in the US are convicted felons.

The Gospel Prophecy

Jesus followed these predictions with an amazing statement, "And this gospel of the kingdom will be preached in all the world as a witness to all the nations, and then the end will come."[9]

---

[8] news.uga.edu/total-us-population-with-felony-convictions
[9] Matthew 24:14

We are living in the 21st century and its easy for us to see that the message of Christianity and the Bible has spread to many places across the globe. But it's interesting that just three years prior to Jesus making this prediction, He was still relatively unknown. He was known as a carpenter from Nazareth[10]- a very small town in Judea (now called Israel)- a very small area in the Roman empire.

It's sort of like someone living in Amarillo, Texas saying, "My message is going to spread to every nation on earth." And this was long before planes, trains, telephones or the internet, at a time when the fastest mode of transportation was a horse. The claim that Jesus' message would "be preached in all the world as a witness to all the nations" must have sounded to many like quite a boast. Has anyone else in human history ever made such a claim and had it come true?

> "My message is going to spread to every nation on earth." Has anyone else in human history ever made such a claim and had it come true?

Smart People Can be Wrong, Too- Very Wrong

You may have heard of Voltaire- a philosopher, historian and free thinker who was a very influential and prolific writer. He is often considered "the father of the Age of Enlightenment" which took place in the 1700's.

In 1776 Voltaire predicted "One hundred years from my day, there will not be a Bible on earth except one that is looked upon by an antiquarian curiosity-seeker."[11] So, according to "the father of the Age of Enlightenment" by the late 1800's, just about the only place anyone would be able to find a Bible would be in an antique shop.

---

[10] Mark 6:3, Matthew 2:23
[11] crossexamined.org/voltaires-prediction-home-and-the-bible-society-truth-or-myth-further-evidence-of-verification/

Voltaire was a smart man. And apparently, from what he could see, based on the number of people in his day who owned Bibles or were interested in the message of the Bible, Christianity and the Bible were going to fade into oblivion. He predicted that 100 years from his day, almost nobody would even own a Bible. And this was more than 1700 years after Jesus had made His prophecy.

> Voltaire predicted "One hundred years from my day, there will not be a Bible on earth except one that is looked upon by an antiquarian curiosity-seeker." As of 2021, between 5 and 7 billion Bibles had been printed.

Even 1700 years after Jesus made His prediction, the idea that the Christian message would achieve world-wide "fame" seemed like a long shot (at least to Voltaire).

Ironically, as it turns out, 100 years after Voltaire made the 100-year prediction, not only had his prediction of the worldwide scarcity of Bibles not come true, but Voltaire's home was being used to print and store Bibles. In fact, some of the high-quality paper he had planned to print his writings on, was used for Bible printing.[12] And it's estimated that as of 2021, between 5 and 7 billion Bibles had been printed,[13] making the Bible- by far the most printed book in human history.

So, Jesus prophesied that "the Gospel (literally- the good news) of His "Kingdom" "will be preached in all the world as a witness to all the nations, and then the end will come."

Jesus here mentions "the end." But He didn't mean that the world's population is going to be wiped out by a nuclear war or a massive meteor or something. Jesus was referring to "the end of the age" that His disciples had asked about- "...

---

[12] crossexamined.org/voltaires-prediction-home-and-the-bible-society-truth-or-myth-further-evidence-of-verification/

[13] www.guinnessworldrecords.com/world-records/best-selling-book-of-non-fiction

what will be the sign of Your coming, and of the end of the age?"[14]

What are the Chances?

So, Jesus made the prediction that "the Gospel (literally-the good news) of His "Kingdom" "will be preached in all the world as a witness to all the nations, and then the end will come." According to Jesus, the preaching of the Gospel in all the world is a significant milestone in the events leading up to Jesus' return to the earth. According to Jesus, "the end of the age" will come right after the Gospel is preached in all the world.[15]

What is "the Gospel" and has it been preached in all the world? Paul the Apostle (an apostle is "one who is sent by God") who became a follower of Jesus after Jesus had died, tells us that the Gospel message, the "good news" is "that Christ died for our sins according to the Scriptures, and that He was buried, and that He rose again the third day according to the Scriptures."[16]

Has this Gospel message been preached "in all the world"? Well, you may be surprised to learn that for many hundreds of years after Christianity began, the Gospel message was not preached in much of the world at all.

While the Gospel spread throughout the Roman Empire fairly quickly, it hadn't gone much farther than Europe and Israel for the first 1,000 years after Jesus lived. The Gospel wasn't preached in China, Japan, North America, South America, or Australia. It wasn't preached around the world. Even after 1900 years of Christianity, many areas of the world had yet to be reached with the "good news" of Jesus Christ.

Many Christians mistakenly think that Jesus was predicting that every person on earth would hear the Gospel

---
[14] Matthew 24:3
[15] In subsequent chapters of this book, we will look at what "the end of the age" will look like.
[16] 1st Corinthians 15:3-4

message before Jesus returns. It's important to notice that Jesus didn't say "This gospel of the kingdom will be preached to every person on earth and then the end will come." He said the Gospel would be preached "in all the world... to all the nations" And as of just recently, for the first time in human history- the Gospel message has now been preached in every nation on earth.

While this prophecy wasn't fulfilled for 1900 years after Jesus made the prediction- today, billions of people have heard the Gospel. The Gospel is being preached in every nation on earth. One ministry alone- Global Media Outreach- has communicated the Gospel message through the internet to more than 2 billion people. Books, eBooks, websites, television, radio and Christian missionaries are reaching many millions of people every day.

> While this prophecy wasn't fulfilled for 1900 years after Jesus made the prediction- today, the Gospel is preached in every nation on earth.

Has any other prophet, mystic, psychic or soothsayer in all of human history ever made such a prediction of future fame and had their prediction be fulfilled? No. Only Jesus.

And can any other generation since the time of Jesus say that this prophecy had been fulfilled? No. And Jesus said, "And this gospel of the kingdom will be preached in all the world as a witness to all the nations, and then the end will come."

After 2,000 years, the Gospel has finally been preached in all the world to all the nations. If Jesus is a true prophet of God- the end of the current world system is coming soon. This may sound like "crazy talk" to you but there are many more fulfilled prophecies and even far more amazing prophecies in the Bible that prove that what the Bible says really is a message from the one True and Living God- and that time is short. Since you may not be 100% convinced yet, let's look at more proof- because there is a lot more.

You might be thinking, "Ok, so Jesus made a number of prophecies 2,000 years ago, and it seems like they are all being fulfilled exactly as He predicted they would be. But it's not enough to convince me that the Bible is 'God-breathed' and that I need to take it seriously."

There's More, Much More

Whether or not you at this point are amazed by the fulfillment of these prophecies of Jesus, or whether you think this small-town carpenter just got really, really "lucky" in His guesses, it is noteworthy that the predictions we've looked at so far are all contained in just a couple of paragraphs of what Jesus said when He was on the earth. He made many more prophecies and as we've mentioned, there are over 1,000 prophecies of the Bible that have been fulfilled precisely as they were predicted to be fulfilled.

Since at this point, you may or may not be 100% convinced that Jesus received direct communication from the God who created the universe, we will give you more evidence. Because there is more, much more. After all, if as we are claiming, the Bible is a communication from the God who created the universe, then surely there should be lots of proof, right? There is. And if you are brave enough to keep looking at the evidence, we will see that the proof is undeniable.

7

Looking Back to See Forward

"Declaring the end from the beginning ..."
- Isaiah 46:10

The evidence we have been examining so far is from the New Testament (written after Jesus was crucified) but some of the Bible's most amazing predictions are recorded in the Old Testament (written hundreds of years before Jesus was born).

The Exact Day Predicted 600 Years in Advance

One of the many events in History that was amazingly and precisely predicted in the Bible, was the exact day that Jesus (the Jewish Messiah) would enter Jerusalem riding on a donkey,[1] the "triumphal entry." The prophet Daniel, writing about 550 BC wrote, "Know therefore and understand, that from the going forth of the command to restore and build Jerusalem until Messiah the Prince, there shall be seven weeks and sixty-two weeks..."[2]

The word "week" in our English Bibles is actually "seven" in the Hebrew language of the Old Testament. The word was used like we use the word "decade"- which means "ten," but we use it to mean "ten years." So, Daniel said there would be "seven weeks and sixty-two weeks," or "seven sevens and sixty-two sevens." That equals 69 weeks (sevens). Sixty-nine x 7 years = 483 years. (Daniel used the Babylonian calendar,

---

[1] Zechariah 9:9
[2] Daniel 9:25

which had a 360-day year.[3]) It adds up to 483 x 360 = 173,880 days. Nehemiah 2:1-8 tells us that King Artaxerxes gave the command to restore and rebuild Jerusalem in (the month of Nisan in) 444 BC.[4]

Did anything noteworthy happen 173,880 days after the day Artaxerxes issued the decree to rebuild Jerusalem?[5] Yes, according to many scholars, that is the day Jesus rode into Jerusalem on a donkey and was welcomed as the King of Israel.[6] According to analysis of the Biblical record and astrological charts, that was on Palm Sunday, March 29th, AD 33 and a week later, on April 3rd, AD 33 Jesus was crucified.[7]

It's amazing that almost 600 years in advance, the Old Testament predicted the exact day that Jesus would enter Jerusalem and be welcomed as King.[8] Let's look at some prophecies that have been fulfilled more recently.

Another one of many amazing predictions in the Bible is in the book of Ezekiel, which was written almost 600 years before Jesus was born. Ezekiel records some amazing predictions that have been fulfilled in recent years.

---

[3] Also, Genesis 7:11, 8:3, 4 shows 150 days = 5 months. And Revelation 11:2-3 and 12:6-14 show 1,260 days, 42 months, and 3.5 years are equivalent- Thus Genesis and Revelation also point to 360-day years.

[4] We know the time of King Artaxerxes' rule through numerous historical and archeological sources.

[5] chrome-extension://efaidnbmnnnibpcajpcglclefindmkaj/https://digitalcommons.liberty.edu/cgi/viewcontent.cgi?article=1208&context=eleu

[6] Matthew 21:1-17; Mark 11:1-11; Luke 19:29-40; John 12:12-19

[7] Scholars differ in their findings regarding the exact date of the crucifixion, but two analyses are offered here- www.researchgate.net/publication/265114769_The_Jewish_Calendar_A_Lunar_Eclipse_and_the_Date_of_Christ%27s_Crucifixion **and** cbs.mbts.edu/2020/04/08/april-3-ad-33-why-we-believe-we-can-know-the-exact-date-jesus-died

[8] Since the Bible precisely predicted the exact year and month of the fulfillment, we are giving it the benefit of doubt that it also predicted the exact day (173,880 days from the command to restore Jerusalem).

Israel Scattered and Regathered- 1,900-Years Later

As mentioned earlier, an astounding 8,352 verses in the Bible contain predictions of future events. Of these, 6,641 verses are in the Old Testament.[9] In order to keep this book from being too long, we are just going to look at a few Old Testament prophecies. Several Old Testament prophets had told the Israelites that if they obeyed God, they would be blessed greatly, but also warned them that if they disobeyed God, He would bring judgment on them. For example, Moses warned the Israelites "But it shall come to pass, if you do not obey the voice of the LORD your God, to observe carefully all His commandments and His statutes which I command you today, that all these curses will come upon you and overtake you."[10] And he specifically warned them, "Then the LORD will scatter you among all peoples, from one end of the earth to the other"[11]

Not only did several Old Testament prophets warn of the possible scattering of the Israelites, but Jesus also predicted that God's warning to the Jewish people would be fulfilled- because the majority of the people of Israel rejected Jesus as being the Savior who the prophets said God would send them. Jesus prophesied of the coming dispersion of the Jewish people, saying, "And they will fall by the edge of the sword, and be led away captive into all nations."[12]

But Ezekiel had also prophesied that God would later regather the people of Israel from all the nations. Ezekiel quotes God as saying, "Thus says the Lord GOD: 'Surely I will take the children of Israel from among the nations, wherever they have gone, and will gather them from every side and

---

[9] Encyclopedia of Biblical Prophecy, J. Barton Payne, pg. 13
[10] Deuteronomy 28:15
[11] Deuteronomy 28:64. Note: The Jews were taken captive into Babylon and again exiled from the land in AD 70.
[12] Luke 21:24

bring them into their own land; and I will make them one nation in the land.'"[13]

The prophet Jeremiah also predicted that the people of Israel would be regathered from across the world. He said, "Thus speaks the LORD God of Israel, saying: 'Write in a book for yourself all the words that I have spoken to you. For behold, the days are coming,' says the LORD, 'that I will bring back from captivity My people Israel and Judah,' says the LORD. 'And I will cause them to return to the land that I gave to their fathers, and they shall possess it.'"[14]

> Exactly as the Bible predicted- the people of Israel were scattered across the earth, and 1900 years later, exactly as the Bible predicted- Israel became a nation.

Just as the Bible predicted, almost all of the Jewish people were driven out of their homeland in AD 70. But in the late 1800's, Jewish people started moving back to the land of Israel. Due to their persecution in numerous countries and especially after Hitler's genocide of the Jews (as well as many Christians, blacks and homosexuals), the numbers increased and just as God had promised, the Jews have been drawn back to the land of their forefathers.

On May 14th, 1948, Israel became a nation. It's noteworthy that prior to their dispersion, the Israelites had been living in two separate kingdoms (northern and southern), but when the Israelites were gathered back into the land, just as Ezekiel specifically predicted, for the first time in history, they became "one nation in the land."[15]

---

[13] Ezekiel 37:21-22; see also: Ezekiel 36:24
[14] Jeremiah 30:2-3 While this prophecy was partially fulfilled earlier, it also refers to a "the latter days" regathering of Israel- as we can see in verse 24- "In the latter days you will consider it (or "understand it")."
[15] Ezekiel 37:22

A Long Time to Be Away from Home

This prophecy was fulfilled about 2,500 years after Ezekiel made the prophecy and 1,900 years after the Jewish people were driven out of their land. Never in recorded history had there been a people group who left their homeland and yet remained a distinct people group for more than about 100 years. And it wasn't just for 100, 200, 500 or even 1,000 years, but for almost 2,000 years after being driven out of their land, the Jewish people had still not assimilated into other people groups.

After 1,878 years (AD 70 to 1948)- the scattered Jews became a nation. Against all odds, as of today, more than 3,300,000 Jews from many countries have returned to "the promised land" of Israel- precisely as the Bible predicted they would.[16] And the vast majority of these Jews are not religious, so they are not intentionally trying to fulfill a Bible prophecy. And even now, at the time of the writing of this book, Jewish people are leaving other countries and returning to the land of Israel- just like the Bible said they would- almost 2,600 years ago.

When did the God of the Bible say the regathering of Israel would happen? In "the latter days"[17] (or "the last days").

Was this specific prediction an amazing fulfillment of the scattering and regathering of the people of Israel after 1900 years of dispersion, just one more "lucky guess" by the prophets in the Bible? In case you think it was, let's consider another prophecy of the Old Testament prophets. And if you are honest, I think you'll have to admit- this one is amazing.

Jerusalem to be "a Heavy Stone" for the Nations

Around 500 BC, the Old Testament prophet Zechariah made a number of predictions that have amazingly come true. In one of Zechariah's prophecies about the end times, he

---

[16] https://evidenceunseen.com/apologetics/predictive-prophecy/the-regathering-of-israel
[17] Jeremiah 30:24

quoted God as saying, "Behold, I will make Jerusalem a cup of drunkenness to all the surrounding peoples, when they lay siege against Judah and Jerusalem. And it shall happen in that day that I will make Jerusalem a very heavy stone for all peoples; all who would heave it away will surely be cut in pieces, though all nations of the earth are gathered against it."[18] (A note of clarification regarding the word "all" in the Bible. While many of us think of the word "all" as meaning the same as the word "every"- in the Bible, the word "all" can carry a more general meaning, as in "basically all," so Zechariah is not necessarily predicting that "every single nation" or "every single person" will be against Israel.)

The tiny nation of Israel is a little larger than New Jersey. It's about 1/6th the size of Florida. But Israel is the subject of more United Nations condemnations than all the other nations on earth combined- by far. From 2012 through 2015, the United Nations General Assembly adopted a total of 97 resolutions criticizing countries; 83 of them have been against Israel- that's 86% of the UN General Assembly's condemnations.[19] And from 2015 up to March of 2025, the UN General Assembly issued 170 condemnations against tiny Israel, only 12 against Syria, 10 against North Korea, 9 against Iran, 9 against Myanmar and zero against China.[20] That is an amazing statistic- especially when you consider the genocide and vast number of human rights violations committed by these other nations.

> The nation of Israel is a little bit bigger than New Jersey. It's about 1/6th the size of Florida. But Israel is the subject of more United Nations condemnations than all the other nations on earth combined- by far.

The UN General Assembly consistently fails to issue condemnations of China (or Syria, North Korea, Iran or Myanmar), but according to the Council

---

[18] Zechariah 12:2-3
[19] unwatch.org/un-israel-key-statistics
[20] unwatch.org/database

on Foreign Relations, "The Chinese government imprisoned more than one million Uyghur people between 2017 and 2022, and subjected those not detained to intense surveillance, religious restrictions, forced labor, and forced sterilizations. The United States determined that China's actions constitute genocide."[21] But for some reason, out of all the nations in the world, the UN is fixated on issuing condemnations against Israel. Just as Zechariah's prophecy about the last days predicted, Jerusalem is "a very heavy stone for all peoples."

Not Just the People- the Place

Amazingly, the 2,500-year-old prophecy of Zechariah is not just about Israel. It specifically mentions Jerusalem. Jerusalem at the time Zechariah made the prophecy was about ¼th of a square mile in size. That's very small. There is a shopping mall in Dubai today that is almost twice as big as Jerusalem was when Zechariah made his prophecy.[22] And yet Jerusalem is at the epicenter of a tremendous amount of conflict. Zechariah said it would be a "a very heavy stone for all peoples." And for those who know about the desires of hundreds of millions of radical Muslims around the world, it doesn't take a stretch of the imagination to see that Jerusalem could be the epicenter of a soon-coming Biblically predicted conflict involving many nations.[23]

A skeptic reading this might say, "Well, of course Jerusalem is a source of conflict for nations around the world- the Jews and the Muslims both lay claim to the temple mount in Jerusalem as well as to the land of Israel." That's true but keep in mind- Zechariah made his prediction over 1,000 years before Islam even existed. In Zechariah's day, there was no dispute over the land of Israel, and nobody whatsoever was

---

[21] www.cfr.org/backgrounder/china-xinjiang-uyghurs-muslims-repression-genocide-human-rights
[22] travelwithliya.com/travel-tips/the-largest-shopping-malls-in-the-world
[23] Ezekial 38-39

arguing about who had the rights to the temple mount in Jerusalem. In the days of Zechariah, Israel didn't even have a king.

Twenty-five hundred years ago, out of the 57 million square miles of land on the earth, a Jewish prophet picked the exact ¼th of a square mile of the earth where this prophecy would be precisely fulfilled. Is there any other ¼th of a square mile on earth that comes anywhere close or has ever come anywhere close to fulfilling a prediction like this? No. But just as the prophet Zechariah predicted 2,500 years ago, Jerusalem is "a very heavy stone for all peoples." Nations around the world are concerned and are trying to find answers for the dilemma of the "heavy stone" of Jerusalem.

And when does the Bible predict these events would take place? Right before the return of the Messiah- "... then they will look on Me whom they pierced. Yes, they will mourn for Him as one mourns for his only son, and grieve for Him as one grieves for a firstborn."[24]

Nations Aligning for an Invasion of Israel

As mentioned at the beginning of this book, we are examining Bible prophecies that pertain mostly to what the Bible calls, "the latter days"[25] or "the last days."[26] And again, these are events that the Bible predicts will lead up to "the end of the age,"[27] when there will be radical changes- even "the end of the world as we know it."[28]

Another last days prophecy made 2,500 years ago by the prophet Ezekiel was that "in the latter days"[29] there will be a group of nations that align in an effort to invade Israel. This group of nations will include Russia, Iran, Turkey and Libya.

---

[24] Zechariah 12:10; See also- Psalm 22 (especially verse 16) and Isaiah 53
[25] Ezekiel 38:16
[26] Acts 2:17
[27] Matthew 24:3
[28] We will explore what that will look like a bit later in this book.
[29] Ezekiel 38:16

Other nations that are part of the "Gog-Magog" alliance include Northern Sudan and other Muslim majority former Soviet Union countries. Ezekiel refers to these countries by their ancient names, but many scholars agree about the modern names of these nations.[30]

According to Ezekiel, these nations will be led by Russia.[31] Ezekiel tells us, "God says, to Gog, (the Russian leader) 'I will turn you around, put hooks into your jaws, and lead you out, with all your army,'"[32] and says, "In the latter years you will come into the land of those brought back from the sword and gathered from many people on the mountains of Israel, which had long been desolate; they were brought out of the nations, and now all of them dwell safely. You will ascend, coming like a storm, covering the land like a cloud, you and all your troops and many peoples with you."[33]

Looking at that prophecy, we see several things. First, it will happen after the people of Israel are regathered in the land of Israel. Secondly, it will be at a time when Israel is at peace that this alliance of nations will invade. Thirdly, God says to the leader, He will "put hooks into your jaws and lead you out." The leader of Russia will be pulled into the invasion of Israel.

Like some other Bible prophecies, at first glance this may not sound all that profound. But consider this- in all of recorded human history, for thousands of years- Russia, Iran and Turkey have never been allies. But in the last few years, for the first time in

> **For the first time in recorded history, Russia, Iran and Turkey are forming partnerships. And they are all opposed to Israel.**

---

[30] There is general agreement as to the identity of these nations although some scholars differ slightly on the names of a few of them.
[31] While there isn't complete agreement among scholars that this is Russia, Ezekiel three times mentions them as being in the "far north" (Ezekiel 38:6,15; 39:2) which is where Russia is relative to Israel.
[32] Ezekiel 38:4
[33] Ezekiel 38:8-9

recorded history, Russia, Iran and Turkey are forming partnerships. Iran sold weapons (drones, etc.) to Russia during Russia's war with Ukraine and in January of 2025 Russia and Iran signed a treaty designed to last 20 years- covering a wide range of issues, from energy, finance and counterterrorism to combating money laundering and organized crime. In fact, in March of 2025, Russia and Iran (along with China) conducted joint military drills in the middle east.[34]

Turkey has become increasingly expansionist in recent years, and Turkey's president Erdogan made a statement recently, saying "There are currently only two leaders left in the world - there is me and there is Vladimir Putin."[35]

Other than Russia, the nations listed by Ezekiel are all predominately Muslim. There may likely soon be a military offensive by these Muslim led nations to once and for all- deal with their mutual dislike of Israel and the Jewish people and to gain control of the land of Israel and the temple mount in Jerusalem.

At this point, we can only guess what the "hooks in the jaws" might be that will be used to draw the leader of Russia to want to invade Israel, but it is noteworthy that as of the time of the writing of this book, it is being reported in the news that the Ukraine war has severely impacted the Russian economy. And in recent years, Israel has made some of the world's largest discoveries of natural gas and oil.

In 2010 a discovery named Leviathan was the world's largest discovery of natural gas in a decade. Israel's infrastructure minister called this discovery "the most important energy news since the founding of the state." This discovery came just a year after the Tamar discovery, which was the world's largest natural gas discovery in 2009- with an estimated 13.17 trillion cubic feet of natural gas (estimated to be worth more than $80B). There is also a large shale oil

---
[34] www.jpost.com/international/article-845658
[35] The Associated Press- December 19, 2024

deposit 30 miles west of Jerusalem. These deposits comprise the third largest shale oil reserve in the world and are expected to yield 250-500 billion barrels of oil. At current oil prices, that amounts to between 16 and 26 trillion dollars. Many experts believe that Israel has a volume of oil in this reserve and other undiscovered shale oil reserves equivalent to that of Saudi Arabia.[36] That's not bad for a nation the size of New Jersey. Needless to say, tens of trillions of dollars worth of oil and gas deposits may end up being a hook in the jaw of financially strapped Russia.

What are the Chances?

We can look at world events- the advance of Islam and the discoveries of oil and natural gas in Israel and we can say, "Well, yes, obviously, these events may converge and result in a group of nations including Russia, Iran, Turkey and Libya- invading Israel. But again, for a man living 2,500 years ago in a tiny little kingdom the size of New Jersey, to be able to accurately predict the precise alignment of nations against tiny Israel, that is to take place "in the latter days?" Do you believe this is all just coincidence?

This book is making the claim that the Bible is a message from God to humanity and that everyone needs to put their trust in the God of the Bible. Obviously, putting one's trust in a book is not something that should be entered into lightly. So, let's look at more evidence. Can we conclusively say that the God of the Jews and Christians wrote the Bible and He proved it by telling us the future in advance? Let's look and see if the Bible really does provide definitive proof.

---

[36] www.dglaw.co.il/oil-and-gas-exploration-in-israel

Prophecies to be fulfilled before Jesus returns to the earth:
1- A dramatic increase in war-
    Being fulfilled in the last 100 years
2- A dramatic increase in famines-
    Being fulfilled in the last 100 years
3- A dramatic increase in pestilences-
    Being fulfilled in the last 100 years
4- A dramatic increase in earthquakes-
    Being fulfilled in our lifetime
5- Worldwide persecution of Christians
    Fulfilled in the last 100 years
6- Israel regathered and becomes a nation-
    Fulfilled May 14, 1948
7- Jerusalem "a heavy stone" for the nations-
    Fulfilled- in our lifetime
8- The formation of a one world government-
    Being Fulfilled- in our lifetime
9- The rise of a united Europe-
    Fulfilled- in our lifetime
10- Nations aligning for Israel "Gog-Magog" invasion-
    Being fulfilled- in our lifetime
11- The Gospel preached in all nations-
    Fulfilled- in our lifetime"

The above list is just a partial list of the last days prophecies that the Bible says would be fulfilled before Jesus returns to the earth. Let's look at a few of the Bible's most amazing last days prophecies.

8

An Amazing Prophecy

"Call to Me, and I will answer you, and show you great and mighty things, which you do not know."
- Jeremiah 33:3

    You may be familiar with what's commonly called the UPC- The universal product code. This is the barcode that is found on most products that we all buy. If you are being honest (which is very important in this situation), you will have to admit that (in addition to all of these other fulfilled prophecies) - if 2,000 years ago, the Bible accurately indicated the use of the UPC for buying and selling, that the Bible is indeed not "just another book" written by people who claim to know the future.

    If a man writing a letter while imprisoned on a tiny island in the Mediterranean Sea 2,000 years ago, who claimed that God gave him a vision of the end times, if this man could accurately indicate the modern use computer barcodes, then you need to admit it- the Bible is a communication from the True and Living God. It simply cannot be that by chance, some elderly guy sitting on a rock, dressed in a robe could somehow come up with this on his own.

    You might be thinking, "Ok, yeah, right. Prove it."
Ok. The book of Revelation is the last book in the Bible. While many people think Revelation is a difficult book to understand; there are passages in the Bible that clearly provide the information needed to rightly interpret the symbolism in the book. And much of the book of Revelation

is written in a very straightforward, obvious and chronological manner.

While many people (even many Christians) like to believe that the last days prophecies of Revelation are figurative and are not meant to be taken literally (they believe that when Revelation says, "1,000 years" – that God really doesn't mean 1,000 years), it is noteworthy that the hundreds of Bible prophecies about past events including Jesus' first coming were fulfilled literally- not figuratively. The Bible meant what it said.

There is no valid reason to think that regarding the return of Christ and other last days events, that God would suddenly switch to speaking in vague terms that don't mean what they say. (Why would God leave everyone guessing as to what He really means?) God is the Master communicator. He means what He says. Unless a Bible verse is clearly symbolic or figurative, it should be interpreted literally.[1]

We will be looking at some of the predictions in Revelation that reveal the events that will be taking place on earth soon, but first, let's look at the claim that the UPC barcode is indicated in this book.

John, an Apostle[2] of Jesus wrote the book and foretold of a coming world leader who the Bible refers to in several ways, including- "the Antichrist,"[3] "the man of sin ... the son of perdition [destruction],"[4] "the lawless one"[5] and "the beast."[6] John also tells us that there will be a man who comes on the

---

[1] For example, the Bible speaks of "the four corners of the earth" but that is clearly figurative, as the Bible teaches that the world is round- Isaiah 40:22. See- https://creation.com/en/articles/isaiah-40-22-circle-sphere
[2] One who is "sent" by God
[3] 1 John 2:18
[4] 2 Thessalonians 2:3
[5] 2 Thessalonians 2:8
[6] Revelation 13:2

scene who will promote the Antichrist. He is referred to as "another beast"[7] and is called "the false prophet."[8]

The Universal Product Code

In Revelation chapter 13, John tells us that this false prophet will be able to perform signs and wonders in order to deceive people all around the world and says, "He causes all, both small and great, rich and poor, free and slave, to receive a mark on their right hand or on their foreheads, and that no one may buy or sell except one who has the mark or the name of the beast, or the number of his name. Here is wisdom. Let him who has understanding calculate the number of the beast, for it is the number of a man: His number is 666."[9]

This is where it really gets interesting. The Bible tells us that the false prophet will cause people all over the world "to receive a mark on their right hand or on their foreheads" and that nobody will be able to "buy or sell" unless they have received this mark on their bodies ("on their right hand or on their foreheads"). What is the mark? The Bible tells us that it involves the number 666.

Two thousand years ago when this prediction was made, this must have sounded bizarre. "What? Nobody on earth will be able to buy or sell unless they have a '666' on their right hand or forehead?"

Fast forward to today. Almost every product in almost every store in almost every nation on earth has the UPC barcode on it.[10]

---

[7] Revelation 13:11
[8] Revelation 19:20
[9] Revelation 13:16-18
[10] Products sold as part of a larger package, handmade items and produce typically don't have individual UPCs.

Take a moment to pick up (almost) anything (other than produce) you bought in a store, and you'll see it. We've all heard the little beep the scanner makes when we are at the checkout counter. In fact, most of us have heard that beep thousands or tens of thousands of times. How does it work? Well, the scanner finds the UPC barcode's "guide bars" and reads the numbers (encoded using a unique pattern of bars and spaces within the barcode) in between those three pairs of guide bars.

The guide bars are two long thin lines which represent the number "6" to a scanner. There are three of these sixes on every UPC barcode- one at the beginning, one in the middle and one at the end of the barcode. As you look at the product, look at the bottom of the barcode. Do you see the three long pairs of thin lines extending below the length of most of the other bars? UPC barcodes include information such as product identity, size, weight, manufacturer, information about the facility where the product was manufactured, etc.[11]

As you can see from the barcodes pictured here, both the Universal Product Code (UPC-12) and the International Article Number (EAN-13) (formerly called the "European Article Number") use the 666 guide bars.

While UPC codes are not legally required, if you go to a store today, it will be difficult to "buy or sell" without using the 666 UPC barcode. Just try to tell the cashier at Costco, Walmart or any store you shop at, that you'd like to purchase all your items without using the UPC barcode (and ask them not to use it either). You will make things quite difficult for the cashier.

---

[11] www.barcodelookup.com/symbology

The Most Amazing Prophecy and So What? 77

And chances are, if you go into almost any store in almost any nation on earth, you will face the same difficulty.

Is it just another amazing coincidence that 2,000 years ago, the Bible predicted that there will be a time when you will not be able to "buy or sell" things anywhere on earth without the number 666? Do you believe it's really just a coincidence that most products (trillions of them) in most of the stores on the planet have the number 666 on them? Do you believe this is just another coincidence, along with all of the fulfilled prophecies we've looked at so far in this book?

The Skeptic's Response

"But wait!" the skeptic says. "I don't need to take a mark on my right hand or forehead before I go shopping, so that prophecy has definitely not been fulfilled!" Ok, we'll give one point to the skeptic on that one (or maybe 666 points).

But let's be honest about this prophecy. How far away do you think we are from seeing that prophecy being able to be fulfilled?

First of all, as we've pointed out, almost every store in almost every country on earth has the number 666 on almost every product. Do you think that's just a coincidence? Or do you think it might just be a giant conspiracy conceived and carried out by thousands of Christians over many years in many countries in order to make it look like the Bible

> Is it just another coincidence that 2,000 years ago, the Bible predicted that there will be a time when you will not be able to "buy or sell" things without the number 666?

is true- even though most of the people involved in developing and implementing the use of the UPC barcode over the years weren't even Christians?

Modern Convenience- A Tool of the Antichrist?

If you've lived more than a couple of decades, you have no doubt noticed that more and more purchases are being made with credit cards and other digital methods of payment, and less and less purchases are being made with cash. The world is increasingly moving towards a cashless economy, driven by technological advancements, consumer preferences, and even the recent COVID-19 pandemic. Digital payments like mobile wallets and contactless cards are becoming increasingly popular. According to a 2024 survey, "Roughly nine in ten consumers in both the United States and Europe report having made some form of digital payment over the past year, with the United States reaching a new high at 92 percent."[12]

The trend is accelerating in the US and globally as well. In Norway, 97% of consumers use digital methods to pay for their shopping, according to a survey by Norway's central bank. In Sweden, 90% of purchases are digital and other European nations are not too far behind. In 2024, "almost 164 billion digital payments were recorded across India. This was a significant increase compared to the previous three years."[13]

In China- "Mobile payment platforms dominate, with a combined user base exceeding 1.3 billion individuals, accounting for nearly the entire adult population."[14]

In fact, even Japan, a country that has traditionally resisted the trend toward a cashless economy, is now moving toward digital payments. Japan hosted the World Expo 2025- an event that was hailed as the first entirely cashless world's fair.[15] Approximately 28 million people at one event- spending not one cent (or 1 yen) of cash.

---

[12] www.mckinsey.com/industries/financial-services/our-insights/banking-matters/state-of-consumer-digital-payments-in-2024
[13] www.statista.com/statistics/1251321/india-total-volume-of-digital-payments
[14] www.linkedin.com/pulse/copy-china-leads-way-cashless-future-analysis-adoption-yee-chun-lim-gbtec
[15] www.expo2025.or.jp/en/cashless

What's the Big Deal About Digital Currency?

Digital purchasing is a convenient way to buy things. Why handle cash which could be dirty (and will likely get some increased press coverage soon as a potential carrier of dangerous diseases)? Digital purchasing makes sense. No doubt. Just scan a card over a reader in almost any store (or scan your hand at over 500 Whole Foods or Amazon stores) and presto, the purchase is completed. No counting change. No dirty cash. It's so simple and makes so much sense.

We are not saying that digital purchasing is bad, but let's consider this trend in the light of Bible prophecy. Let's assume for a minute that the Bible is the communication from God to humanity. Let's assume that the Bible's warning is true regarding a soon-coming world leader who will require people to take a digital "666" on their right hand or forehead in order "to buy or sell."

What would that look like? The Bible predicts that the 666 will be a "mark." The original language that the prophecy was written in (ancient Greek) uses the word "charagma"- it could be translated in English as "an imprinted mark, a stamp or an engraving." Based on the fact that it will involve the number 666 and that it will be needed for buying and selling, in our modern age of putting barcodes on products and implanting microchips into pets, it is very easy to imagine that the "mark" may be a tiny, implanted microchip or maybe more likely- an invisible tattoo with a barcode in it.

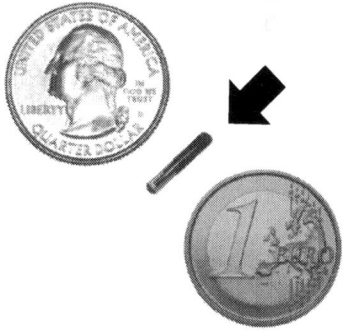

Technology is changing rapidly, so we don't know for sure what form it will take, but the step from the world's current practice of putting a 666 on almost every product sold on the planet, to also putting a 666 on every person buying the products- is not a very big step.

A Barcode for Bowser

Back in the 1980's it became possible to get microchips injected into our pets. It's a great way to get Bowser back if he runs away and someone finds him across town- even if his collar with his nametag falls off. When someone finds Bowser looking lost, a quick scan of his microchip and shazam! You get Bowser returned to your loving care.

But as time has passed, having microchips inserted into pets isn't just a convenience. In many places- it's the law. In Hawaii for example, where I live, "in 2020, the City & County of Honolulu replaced the dog licensing system with rules requiring that all pet dogs 3 months and older and cats 4 months and older must have microchip identification."[16]

The microchipping of Bowser and Fluffy is no longer just a convenience; the penalty for the "crime" of not having a microchip implanted in Bowser or Fluffy could cost you quite a bit. The penalty for not having Bowser microchipped on O'ahu can include a fine of up to $1,000 and imprisonment for up to 30 days, or both.[17]

In the UK, the penalty for the "crime" of not having implanted Bowser or Fluffy could cost you $676.81.[18] Microchipping of pets is also mandatory in European Union nations as well as in Japan, New Zealand, Israel and parts of Australia.

In many places, barcode implants for your pets are no longer just a good idea- if you don't do it- you are breaking the law. But in case you are worried that your Bowser or Fluffy has accidentally received "the mark of the beast," rest assured- they haven't. The barcodes currently injected into pets do not use the "666" type of barcodes.

---

[16] www.hawaiianhumane.org/pet-identification
[17] codelibrary.amlegal.com/codes/honolulu/latest/honolulu/0-0-0-7766
[18] (Conversion rate as of 9/1/25)

A Barcode for Bob?

Is the idea of having "convenient" microchips put into or onto people- just a far-off distant possibility? No, in fact it's a currently available option. The "Human microchipping market is estimated to be valued at $1.96 billion in 2025 and is expected to reach $3.15 billion in 2032."[19]

Tens of thousands of people around the world have already chosen this convenience. In fact, it's becoming so common, that "U.S. states are increasingly enacting legislation to preemptively ban employers from forcing workers to be 'microchipped,' which entails having a subdermal chip surgically inserted between one's thumb and index finger.

"Internationally, more than 50,000 people have elected to receive microchip implants to serve as their swipe keys, credit cards, and means to instantaneously share social media information. This technology is especially popular in Sweden, where chip implants are more widely accepted to use for gym access, e-tickets on transit systems, and to store emergency contact information."[20]

While there are many emerging technologies that could lead to the "convenience" of a global digital ID, "There are two main types of microchips: one type is the radio-frequency identification (RFID) chips and near field communication (NFC) chips. RFID chips are identifying transponders that generally carry a unique identification number and can be tagged with user data such as health records, social media profiles, and financial information. In contrast, NFC chips use electromagnetic radio fields to wirelessly communicate to

---

[19] www.coherentmarketinsights.com/market-insight/human-microchipping-market-5816

[20] www.carnegiecouncil.org/media/article/preemptive-bans-human-microchip-implants (accessed 9/1/25)

nearby digital readers, like smartphones and contactless credit cards."[21]

Whatever the technology is that becomes "the law," according to the Bible, there will be a time when everyone on earth will need to receive "the mark of the beast" in order to buy or sell. Imagine the convenience- people won't need to have their wallet or purse or even an ID with them when they go to the store- all they need to have with them is their right hand or forehead- the ultimate in convenience. Nobody will ever lose it or forget it at home- and people will no doubt be able to unlock their doors and start their cars with them as well. Nobody will get locked out of their cars or houses.

> Imagine the convenience- people won't need to have their wallet or purse or even an ID with them when they go to the store- all they need to have with them is their right hand or forehead.

There are already some "autonomous" or "cashierless" checkout stores where you can walk in (and quickly scan your phone) and just pick up what you want off the shelves and simply walk out of the store. You walk by the scanner on the way in and since all the products have barcodes on them (and they are tracked using Artificial Intelligence (AI))- you simply walk out of the store, and you are charged automatically.

What's the Big Deal About Digital Identification?

Along the lines of the convenience of digital payments in being able to buy and sell, the concept of everybody on earth being associated with their own specific identifying number is not a far-fetched idea. In the US, we are facing increasing requirements regarding what is considered an acceptable form of identification.

In 2005, the US Congress quietly passed the REAL ID Act, which according to the Department of Homeland Security, "set standards for the issuance of sources of

---

[21] Ibid.

identification, such as driver's licenses and identification cards." According to the law, "Said (REAL ID) cards must also feature specific security features... These cards must also present data in a common, machine-readable format (bar codes, Smart card technology, etc.)." And of course, that involves everyone taking a number.

"REAL ID" Required: "Take a number!"

According to a government website, "As of May 7, 2025, only federal compliant REAL ID driver's licenses and state ID cards will be accepted to get on a domestic airline flight..."[22] The REAL ID Act requires this "enhanced" form of identification be presented (by anyone 18 years of age or older) in order to travel on domestic flights, as well as to enter certain federal facilities. (Regarding international flights- Since 2007, all US Passports issued have an RFID microchip on them.)

It seems people had been reluctant to step up and take a number as the REAL ID deadline for domestic flights, initially set for 2008, had been repeatedly extended, but the enforcement date was finally set as being May 7, 2025.[23]

The "Countdown to REAL ID Enforcement" put out by the U.S. Department of Homeland Security might have seemed a bit threatening to some who had seen it online.

The Department of Homeland Security website-

Countdown to REAL ID Enforcement

43	7	3	14
days	hours	minutes	seconds

Are you REAL ID ready?

---

[22] A US passport or military ID can also be used- www.honolulu.gov/csd/real-id (Accessed 9/1/25)

[23] www.tsa.gov/real-id/about-real-id (Accessed- 6/2/25) (Screenshot from March 24, 2025)

What About People Who Haven't Taken a Number?

At the time of the writing of this book, there are many powerful and influential people working to provide digital IDs for those who live in areas of the world where the long arm of technology hasn't quite reached. And these movers and shakers want to make sure that everyone in the world has a number. In fact, they call digital Identification (i.e.- taking a number) "a fundamental and universal right."[24]

The movers and shakers that have been (or are) involved with this effort include Bill Gates and Microsoft Corporation, the Rockefeller Foundation, Mastercard, the United Nations Foundation and numerous top-level workers in the vaccine industry. The former CEO of GAVI (Global Alliance for Vaccines and Immunizations) was also on the Executive Board of ID2020. ID2020 has now joined with Digital Impact Alliance to help accomplish their goal of the global numbering of people.

According to the homepage of id2020.org- "<u>Digital ID is an essential component</u> of digital public infrastructure ... and enable individuals to access <u>essential government and commercial services</u>." Notice the repeated use of the word, "essential." It seems worth noting that "essential" is not a big step away from "required."[25]

One of the projects of the global ID enterprise was the "Good Health Pass Collaborative." Launched in 2021, "to develop principles and standards for digital health passes aimed at restoring international travel during the COVID-19 pandemic." Some people may find it a bit disturbing that the same people who want to give everyone on earth a number, were also working on "standards for digital health passes" that would be required for travel around the world.

According to the Digital Impact Alliance website, the combining of digital ID and a digital payment system, along

---

[24] www.id2020.org/manifesto
[25] Accessed on March 24, 2025

with "a government commitment to financial inclusion has helped India achieve an 80% financial inclusion rate. And, it has contributed an estimated additional $16.4 billion to their economy."[26]

The main point here is not to say there is an evil "conspiracy" of some kind, to give everyone on earth a number; the main point is to consider the Bible's prediction that a time will come in which people all over the world will not be able to buy or sell unless they have received the new world order's "mark"- the number 666 on their right hand or forehead. For the first time in 2,000 years, this prophecy no longer seems like a far-fetched fantasy. In fact, the fulfillment of this 2,000-year-old prophecy looks like it could be right around the corner.

Benefits Anyone?

You don't need to think very hard in order to come up with a list of possible benefits of having a cashless society along with implanted microchips- or another injected or tattooed digital ID system that could be read by a scanner.

You don't need to believe me on this point, but about 25 years ago, a friend of mine who worked with the military told me he was working with the government to set up a global digital tracking system. From what he said, they planned to implant microchips into people (certain people and their children) so they could use satellites to locate them ("within three meters") anywhere on earth (in case of kidnappings, etc.).

Possible Benefits of Digital ID/Payment Implants:

1) Tracking of people: Having technology that could track or find people could be extremely useful (at the high cost of personal privacy). Think of the security and comfort people could have if their children could be continually tracked and monitored. What about the elderly- "Is Grandpa walking

---

[26] dial.global/work/research

around in the house? Let's look at our phone (or wrist) monitor and see." People with Dementia could be quickly found if they wandered away from home. Employees, students and prisoners could be tracked, as well as parolees and convicted child abusers and sex offenders, etc. People could easily be reconnected with family and friends in the case of natural disasters, etc.

2) Crime prevention and prosecution: If satellites could track everyone (or even facial recognition cameras or scanners on poles [or on people's glasses]- linked with digital ID) think of the amount of crime that could be prevented or at least prosecuted. If a woman was robbed of her wedding ring at 8:00 p.m. last Friday, law enforcement officials could look at the monitoring software, identify who was at the crime scene at the time of the offense and where they are now, and go and arrest them (and maybe even track down where the stolen ring might be.). Imagine how much the murder rate would drop. Think of how much crime could be prevented- there would be no more robberies of cash, money laundering would be difficult (because there would be no cash), and there would be almost no tax evasion (everything would be digitally tracked and calculated). Perpetrators of almost every crime could be found. Who will rob a store or a person when they know they will be caught? People who commit acts of terrorism across the globe could be immediately identified and tracked down. Human trafficking could be almost completely eradicated.

3) Medical Benefits: Microchips could be used to identify patients in hospitals and other healthcare facilities, which could help to improve patient safety and security. The very efficient handling of medical information in emergency rooms could be a lifesaver. Instant identification of unconscious or mentally impaired patients (people with Alzheimer's, Dementia, people on drugs, etc.) and children, etc. could be a game changer- not to mention the benefit of controlling access to restricted areas in healthcare facilities.

4) Convenience: Going cashless – There would be no need to carry "unsafe and unsanitary" cash. There would be no need to carry credit cards and no fear of losing them or having them stolen. Financial transactions would be automatic and instantly recorded and documented. Almost all purchases would be quick and easy.

These benefits would all be easily attainable- if people would just agree to take a "little mark on their right hand or forehead," if they would just agree to follow the charismatic new world order leader and his frontman, the false prophet.

The "ducks are in a row." In most nations on earth, people already need to use the "666" to buy almost everything they purchase in their daily lives. More and more people are moving away from using cash. The Bible predicts that in the future, people will be required to have a 666 on their right hand or forehead in order to make purchases and sales.

If cash was widely used, people could easily circumvent the government's "mark" requirement. It would be easy to make "under the table" cash transactions. But if cash is eventually outlawed and all purchasing is done digitally, with every (legal) purchase being electronically recorded and tracked, it would be much easier to enforce a mandated, "No Mark - No Sale!" policy. Digital currency and digital ID's will be powerful tools in the hands of the new world order, and eventually- the Antichrist.

> Coming soon to all stores near you?
> "No Mark - No Sale!"

"Take a Number!"

As governments all around the world are working to find ways to combat crime and the increase of terrorism, think of what a help the mark could be. Think of how it could help to make peoples' lives "easier and safer."

Amazingly, as we see the nations of the world marching toward cashless/digital currencies, as we see more of the nations of the world embracing digital identification and mass surveillance, as we see a "666" on almost every single product bought and sold on the planet; we can't help but admit that the elderly man sitting on a deserted rocky island 2,000 years ago, didn't just have a vivid imagination when he prophesied that one day, everyone on earth will be required to take a 666 on their right hand or forehead. He had a revelation from the God who says, "Remember the former things of old, for I am God, and there is no other; I am God, and there is none like Me, declaring the end from the beginning, and from ancient times things that are not yet done..."[27]

Will having a mark on everyone's right hand or forehead be convenient and make a lot of sense? Yes. Will having a mark on everyone's right hand or forehead be another amazing fulfillment of Bible prophecy? Yes. Will it be good? Absolutely not. We will see why in an upcoming chapter. And if you are alive on the earth when the mark is being required by the global government/leader, whatever you do - even if it's a matter of life and death - DO NOT TAKE THE MARK!

---

[27] Isaiah 46:10

9

The Most Amazing Prophecy and So What?

> "Therefore the Lord Himself will give you a sign ..."
> - Isaiah 7:14

The fulfilled (and possibly very soon to be fulfilled) prophecies mentioned so far in this book are just a fraction of the Bible's prophecies that have already been fulfilled (or may be on the verge of being fulfilled). Of the 1,817 different prophecies in the Bible, the majority of them have already been fulfilled exactly as predicted.

As we mentioned earlier in this book, in just 35 verses of one chapter of the Bible, the prophet Daniel made 135 prophecies that specifically describe the succession of different rulers of different empires and kingdoms that would take place in the future.[1] There is no way the fulfillment of these prophecies could have happened by chance. And as we looked at in Chapter 7, the day of Jesus' "triumphal entry" into Jerusalem- sitting on the back of a donkey, was predicted almost 600 years before it happened.

The Bible not only predicted the scattering of the people of Israel, but 2,500 years in advance, the Bible predicted that in the last days, Israel would be gathered again and established as one nation- exactly as it was on May 14th, 1948.

The current alienation and singling out of Israel by many world nations, and the first time in history alignment of nations for the coming invasion of Israel, as well as the last

---

[1] Daniel Chapter 11

days use of the number 666 in buying and selling are all clearly predicted by the prophets in the Bible.

Jesus accurately and amazingly predicted events of history and events occurring in the times in which we are now living- and He did it all 2,000 years ago.

Jesus accurately predicted not only the complete destruction of the Jewish temple in Jerusalem, but also described exactly what the multi-ton stone and marble structure would look like- "not one stone shall be left here upon another, that shall not be thrown down."[2]

From the amazingly accurate and specific claim of the dramatic last days increase of intensity and severity of wars, famines, pestilences and earthquakes, to the bold claim that the "good news" of the message of His Kingdom would spread to "all nations," and that the followers of Jesus would be persecuted and killed in nations across the globe- this small town carpenter nailed it every time.

We don't have the space in this book to detail all of the amazingly fulfilled Bible prophecies, so we will look now at the most important and amazing prophecy in the entire Bible.

The Prophecy

The prophecy was that the coming Jewish leader ("Messiah the Prince"[3]) would be killed and then rise from the dead. This prediction was made at least 700 years before Jesus was born. A thorough study of the Old Testament shows that as Jesus said regarding the Old Testament Scriptures, "... they... testify of Me."[4] It could be said that the entire Old Testament points to Jesus. And a central truth in the Old Testament is that the coming

---

[2] Matthew 24:2
[3] Daniel 9:25
[4] John 5:39

Messiah would be a "suffering servant."[5] The message was that He would pay the penalty for the sins of everyone who would put their trust in Him. As Isaiah writes, "All we like sheep have gone astray; we have turned, every one, to his own way; and the LORD has laid on Him the iniquity of us all."[6] And He would be "led as a lamb to the slaughter"[7] and be "cut off from the land of the living."[8] He took our place by taking the penalty we each deserve.

But Isaiah the prophet says that after He is killed, He will continue in life- "He shall prolong His days, and the pleasure of the LORD shall prosper in His hand."[9] King David, another Old Testament prophet, prophesied of Him, saying, "For You will not leave my soul in Sheol [the grave], nor will You allow Your Holy One to see corruption."[10] The idea here is that this "suffering servant" would offer Himself up as a sacrifice for our sins and be killed, but that His body would not decompose in the grave, and in fact- He would rise from the dead.

But the predictions weren't just made by prophets hundreds of years before Jesus was born; Jesus Himself repeatedly predicted His own death and bodily resurrection (rising from the dead),[11] as we are told by Matthew, one of Jesus' disciples (followers)- "... Jesus began to show to His disciples that He must go to Jerusalem, and suffer many things from the elders and chief priests and scribes, and be killed, and be raised the third

> "... Jesus began to show to His disciples that He must go to Jerusalem, and suffer many things from the elders and chief priests and scribes, and be killed, and be raised the third day."

---

[5] Isaiah 53:3-6, 10, 12; Psalm 16:10, Daniel 9:24-26
[6] Isaiah 53:6
[7] Isaiah 53:7
[8] Isaiah 53:8
[9] Isaiah 53:10
[10] Psalm 16:10
[11] John 2:18-22; Matthew 12:39-40; Matthew 16:21

day."[12] (In a moment, we'll look at why we should trust the testimony of Matthew and Jesus' other disciples.)

John, another disciple of Jesus, also records a time when the Jewish leaders who had heard of Jesus performing many miracles, tested Jesus, asking Him to perform a miracle for them, to show them a "sign." "Jesus answered and said to them, 'Destroy this temple, and in three days I will raise it up.' Then the Jews said, 'It has taken forty-six years to build this temple, and will You raise it up in three days?' But He was speaking of the temple of His body. Therefore, when He had risen from the dead, His disciples remembered that He had said this to them; and they believed the Scripture and the word which Jesus had said."[13]

It is a well-established fact that a man named Jesus Christ was publicly executed in Judea in the 1st Century A.D., under the direction of Pontius Pilate (the Roman governor of Judea), by means of crucifixion, at the request of the Jewish Sanhedrin (religious leaders). The non-Christian historical accounts of Flavius Josephus, Cornelius Tacitus, Lucian of Samosata, Maimonides and even the Jewish Sanhedrin (religious leaders who didn't believe that Jesus was the Messiah) all corroborate the early Christian eyewitness accounts of these important historical aspects of the death of Jesus Christ. Many people watched the public crucifixion of Jesus. And they watched Him get stabbed in the side with a spear after He was dead.[14] In order to more fully understand the miracle of Jesus being raised from the dead, it seems that a description of the method of Jesus' execution will be of value.

---

[12] Matthew 16:21
[13] John 2:19-21
[14] John 19:34

The Crucifixion

Before Jesus was crucified, the Roman soldiers brutally beat and scourged Him. A scourge was something like the old British cat o' nine tails, except that the whip was not designed to merely bruise or leave welts on the victim. The scourge was a whip with several (at least three) strands, each possibly as long as three feet, and the strands were weighted with lead balls and/or sharp pieces of bones. This scourge was designed to lacerate. The lead balls or sharp pieces of bone struck the skin so violently that they tore the flesh open.

The church historian Eusebius of Caesarea recounts the detail of a scene of scourging. He says, "For they say that the bystanders were struck with amazement when they saw them lacerated with scourges even to the innermost veins and arteries, so that the hidden inward parts of the body, both their bowels and their members, were exposed to view."[15] After Jesus was beaten, scourged and had a crown of thorns placed on His head, He was then crucified. Scourging often resulted in the death of the victim. Crucifixion always did.

Crucifixion was invented about 500 years before Jesus was born, but it was reportedly "perfected" by the Romans as the most painful way to torture someone to death. It is quite possibly the most painful method of execution ever invented. The English language derives the word "excruciating" from "crucifixion," acknowledging it as a form of slow, painful suffering. The victim of crucifixion was first severely scourged or beaten. He was then forced to carry the large wooden crossbeam to the site of the crucifixion. Bearing this load on his back was extremely painful after the scourging.

When the victim arrived at the place of crucifixion, he would be forced to stretch out his arms on the crossbeam, where they were nailed in place. The nails (possibly 7 to 9 inches long) were hammered through the wrists (not the

---

[15] Ecclesiastical History, Book 4, chapter 15

palms), which kept the nails from pulling through the hand.[16] The placement of the nails in the wrists also caused excruciating pain as the nails pressed on large nerves running into the hands. The crossbeam would then be hoisted up and fastened to an upright post.

After fastening the crossbeam, the executioners would nail the victim's feet to the cross as well- usually one foot on top of the other, nailed through the middle and arch of each foot, with the knees slightly bent. The primary purpose of the nails was to inflict pain.

As mentioned earlier, another prediction about the suffering Messiah, written over 1,000 years before Jesus was born, and about 500 years before crucifixion was invented, describes the cruel death of Jesus, saying, "They pierced My hands and My feet." Have you ever heard of anyone dying from a means that includes having their hands and feet pierced? This prophecy must have sounded bizarre to people for hundreds of years- until crucifixion was invented.

> **"They pierced My hands and My feet." The fact that crucifixion wasn't even invented until 500 years after this prediction was made, makes this prophecy even more amazing.**

And more than a thousand years in advance, it predicted the piercing of Jesus' hands and feet when He was crucified.

Once the victim was fastened to the cross, all his weight was supported by the three nails, which would cause pain to shoot throughout his entire body.

The victim's arms were stretched out in such a way as to cause cramping and paralysis in the chest muscles, making it impossible to inhale. In order to take a breath, the victim had to push up with his feet. In addition to enduring excruciating pain caused by the nail in his feet,

---

[16] In ancient times, the wrist was considered part of the hand.

the victim's lacerated back would rub against the rough upright beam of the cross.

After taking a breath and in order to relieve some of the pain in his feet, the victim would slump down again. This action put his weight on his nailed wrists and again rubbed his shredded back against the cross. However, the victim could not breathe in this lowered position, so the torturous process would begin again; in order to take another breath, the victim would need to again put his weight on the nail in his feet and push up. In either position, the torture was intense and agonizing.

Needless to say, crucifixion was a slow and tortuous death. Death was ultimately by asphyxiation as the victim lost the strength to continue pushing up on his feet in order to take breaths.[17]

Lifeless on the Cross

After He died, as Jesus hung on the cross, we are told that Roman soldiers were ordered to make sure Jesus was dead so they could take His body down from the cross. "Then the soldiers came and broke the legs of the first and of the other who was crucified with Him. But when they came to Jesus and saw that He was already dead, they did not break His legs. But one of the soldiers pierced His side with a spear, and immediately blood and water came out."[18] The "blood and water" are explained by what is called hypovolemic shock (a life-threatening condition that occurs when there is a severe loss of blood or fluid in the body). Prior to death, the sustained rapid heartbeat caused by hypovolemic shock causes fluid to gather in the sack around the heart and around the lungs. This gathering of fluid in the membrane around the heart is called pericardial effusion, and the fluid gathering around the lungs is called pleural effusion.[19] So, in case you

---

[17] www.gotquestions.org/crucifixion.html
[18] John 19:32-34
[19] www.gotquestions.org/blood-water-Jesus.html

are wondering- no, Jesus didn't just faint on the cross. He died on the cross.

The Third Day

But on the morning of the third day after Jesus was brutally beaten, scourged and crucified, there He was again- walking around as alive as ever. In fact, Jesus showed Himself to many people and walked the earth for another 40 days after rising from the dead. And you can be sure that He wasn't limping around like a man who had been tortured (beaten and scourged), been crucified- having large (possibly 7 to 9 inch long) nails driven through His ankles and wrists, had the blood drained out his body- through His back, wrists, ankles and head, and then having been stabbed in His side by a spear.

> On the third day after being publicly crucified, Jesus was able to convince people that He had conquered death. He didn't just faint or "swoon" on that cross- He died. And He rose again.

Jesus didn't just faint or "swoon" or "almost die" from His injuries and then somehow manage to survive and then from the inside of the tomb, roll a two-ton stone away from the entrance of the tomb with His fingertips, somehow getting past a bunch of Roman soldiers who (under the penalty of death) were guarding the tomb to make sure nobody stole the body,[20] and then hobble around town on His pierced ankles for 40 days.

No, on the third day after being publicly crucified, Jesus was able to fully convince everyone who saw Him that He had completely conquered death.

Can you imagine a barely alive man trying to walk around on feet that had been nailed to a cross with 7 to 9 inch nails a day earlier, with huge fresh wounds all over His head, face, side, back, wrists and ankles? That really

---

[20] Matthew 27:62-66

wouldn't have impressed anyone- "Wow, the first person in history to survive a crucifixion! But He sure is a mess! We hope He survives!" No, Jesus was able to convince more than 500 people that He had absolutely conquered death! He had clearly died and was clearly alive and completely well again! Jesus walked the earth for almost a month and a half after He rose from the dead. And He wasn't covered in bandages. The only remaining signs of His crucifixion were His scars.[21] People spent time with Him, touched Him, talked with Him, and even sat down and ate food with Him. How do we know this? Eyewitness testimony.

Are the Witnesses Reliable? Or Are People Willing to Die for a Lie?

Hundreds or thousands of people watched Jesus be publicly crucified. They knew He was dead. And hundreds of people said they saw Him alive again. A lot of them would be persecuted (beaten or tortured, etc.) and some were even killed because they wouldn't deny their claims that they saw Jesus alive after He was crucified.

> Have you ever heard of anyone who was willing to suffer and die for something that they know is a lie?

According to Paul (one of the Apostles of Jesus), there were over 500 eyewitnesses who saw Jesus alive at the same time after He rose from the grave.[22]

Paul said that at the time of his writing about it (about AD 57), most of those eyewitnesses were still alive.[23] If Paul was lying, it would have been an easy thing for people to challenge his testimony- "Really? Five hundred people saw Jesus alive at the same time after He was crucified? Who are these people?" But rather than shrinking to nothing, the number of followers of Jesus grew quickly and dramatically.

---

[21] John 20:26-27
[22] 1 Corinthians 15:6
[23] 1 Corinthians 15:6.

And why would Paul be willing to die for a claim he knew was a lie? You would think that the Christian faith would shrink to nothing after Jesus' death. But instead of Christianity dying out, it grew as Jesus' followers were willing to go to their deaths rather than recant their claims of having seen Jesus alive after His public execution.

Even non-Christians who were alive at the time reported about the Christians being willing to die rather than recant their testimonies about Jesus. For example, Pliny the Elder (Gaius Plinius Secundus (AD 23/24–79) who was a Roman author and naval and army commander wrote to the Roman emperor Trajan, "I have observed the following procedure: I interrogated these as to whether they were Christians; those who confessed I interrogated a second and a third time, threatening them with punishment; those who persisted I ordered executed. For I had no doubt that, whatever the nature of their creed, stubbornness and inflexible obstinacy surely deserve to be punished."[24]

Think about this for a minute. Would you be willing to be beaten, imprisoned and even killed (and maybe have your children killed as well) for something you know is a lie? Do you think other people would be willing to do that? For something they know is a lie? The early followers of Jesus were imprisoned, beaten and killed but they wouldn't deny their claim that they saw Jesus alive and well after His crucifixion. This fact is documented by non-Christian historians alive at the time and more significantly, the fact is supported by the dramatic growth of the number of followers of Jesus after His crucifixion.

---

[24] faculty.georgetown.edu/jod/texts/pliny.html (Pliny's Letters to Trajan X, 97)

Multiplication, Not Subtraction

In the face of intense persecution, if Jesus didn't actually rise from the dead, one would think the number of Jesus' followers would decrease dramatically after He died, but it didn't. When Jesus was arrested by Roman soldiers on the night before His crucifixion, "all the disciples forsook him and fled."[25] All of Jesus' followers ran away.

> Before Jesus was crucified, all of His followers ran away. But within a short time, they were all willing to die rather than recant their testimonies that they saw Him alive again.

Then, on the third day after He was crucified, the followers of Jesus were all gathered in a room, fearing the Jewish leaders who had orchestrated the murder of Jesus.[26] Since they all fit in one room, the number of Jesus' followers might have been between 20 and 30.

Then Jesus appeared to them- alive from the dead. These cowering "followers" were transformed- and they all suddenly became emboldened to the point where they were willing to die for Christ. He talked with them. He ate with them.[27] The number of early followers grew from a couple dozen or so right after the crucifixion, to thousands in less than two months[28] and continued to increase significantly over time.

Do you think those disciples and the 500 other people who saw Him at the same time, were all just imagining things? Do you think those 20 or 30 people could have all had the same hallucinations at the same time? And do you think the 500 other eyewitnesses could have all had the same exact hallucination at the same time as well? Do you think those people who walked with Jesus, talked with Him and even ate with Him after His crucifixion were all just imagining things?

---

[25] Matthew 26:56
[26] John 20:19
[27] Luke 24:41-42
[28] Acts 2:41

If someone told you that there were no buildings destroyed in New York City on September 11th, 2001, would you believe them? No, of course not. Even if you've never been to New York City, in addition to pictures, videos and the physical evidence of the destroyed towers, there are too many eyewitnesses who were there who saw it happen.

But many of the eyewitnesses of the resurrected Jesus, willfully and resolutely endured prolonged torture and death rather than recant their testimonies. This fact attests to their sincerity, ruling out deception on their part.

Why would Jesus' disciples (other than Judas, who betrayed Jesus, precisely as Jesus predicted he would)[29] give up everything they had or could possibly ever have on this earth, to face an executioner's death? Nobody would do that for something they know is a lie. But it wasn't just one person, it was 11 of the 12 disciples of Jesus.[30] And it wasn't just Jesus' close followers. Many people were willing to die rather than deny their claim that they saw Jesus alive after He had been crucified.

> Do you think those 20 or 30 people all had the same hallucinations at the same time? And do you think the 500 other witnesses could all have had the same exact hallucination at the same time as well?

What Do the Experts Say?

Dr. Simon Greenleaf, the famous Professor of Law at Harvard University, produced the famous three-volume work, *A Treatise on the Law of Evidence*, that "is still considered the greatest single authority on evidence in

---

[29] Matthew 26:20-26

[30] John didn't die then. Tertullian (2nd century) wrote that John was "plunged... into boiling oil" but there is no definitive evidence that it happened.

the entire literature of legal procedure."[31] The U.S. judicial system today still relies on the rules of evidence established by Dr. Greenleaf.

Dr. Greenleaf was not a Christian and used to speak against Christianity when he taught law classes at Harvard. Some of his students challenged Dr. Greenleaf to take his three volumes on the laws of legal evidence and apply the principles he taught to the evidence for the resurrection of Jesus. After all, Dr. Greenleaf was the expert.

> After examining the evidence, Dr. Greenleaf came to the conclusion that according to the laws of legal evidence used in courts of law, there is more evidence for the historical fact of the resurrection of Jesus Christ than for just about any other event in history.

The skeptical Dr. Greenleaf accepted their challenge and after examining the evidence for himself, he came to the conclusion that according to the laws of legal evidence used in courts of law, there is more evidence for the historical fact of the resurrection of Jesus Christ than for just about any other event in history.

Writing about the testimony of the writers of the four Gospels (Matthew, Mark, Luke and John), Dr. Greenleaf concluded, "Either the men of Galilee were men of superlative wisdom, and extensive knowledge and experience, and of deeper skill in the arts of deception, than any and all others, before or after them, or they have truly stated the astonishing things which they saw and heard."[32]

Dr. Greenleaf, like so many thousands of others (including many scientists) who have set out to disprove Christianity, came to the conclusion that it is indeed- the truth.

The late jurisprudential prodigy and international statesman Sir Lionel Luckhoo, who holds The Guinness Book

---

[31] Wilber Smith, *Therefore Stand* (Baker Book House, 1973), p. 423
[32] Simon Greenleaf, *Testimony of the Evangelists* (reprint of the 1874 edition, Grand Rapids: Baker Book House, 1984), p. 53

of World Records fame for his unprecedented 245 consecutive defense murder trial acquittals, is another legal expert who examined the evidence for the resurrection. He wrote, "I have spent more than 42 years as a defense trial lawyer appearing in many parts of the world and am still in active practice. I have been fortunate to secure a number of successes in jury trials, and I say unequivocally the evidence for the Resurrection of Jesus Christ is so overwhelming that it compels acceptance by proof which leaves absolutely no room for doubt."[33]

The Bible is the only book written that stakes it's claim to truth on fulfilled prophecy and has about a thousand fulfilled prophecies to prove that its author is God. God in effect says, "This is how you'll know I've written this book. I will tell you history in advance." And again, the thousands of prophecies in the Bible are not vague Nostradamus style prophecies. No other book passes the tests that the Bible does. (More evidence at- www.allaboutGod.com and www.gotquestions.org)

So What?

At this point, you may be saying something like, "Ok, I admit that the Bible is not like other books or prophets, psychics or fortune tellers. The evidence is clear enough for me to make a decision. But what do I need to do?" The Bible clearly teaches that "God is love."[34] That is an absolutely wonderful truth about God. For much of my life, I was an atheist. I didn't believe there was a God who created the universe. I thought that basically, what we can see is all there is to reality. But then I started having spiritual experiences- many of them. I had out-of-body experiences, was spoken to in the Hawaiian language by spirits, I had interactions with UFO's... (this is all written

---

[33] www.gotquestions.org/why-believe-resurrection.html
[34] 1 John 4:8

about in my book, *A Different Life*),[35] but to make a long story short, I came to the place where I realized that I needed to put my trust in Jesus Christ. That was about 35 years ago. In the last 35 years of having a personal relationship with Jesus Christ, if there is one thing I've learned more than anything else about God- it is that God loves us. His love is absolutely amazing.

The Bad News

But we have a problem. God is not only loving, He is also absolutely good, and He is absolutely just- He always does what is morally right. The Bible tells us that "it is appointed for men to die once, but after this the judgment."[36] Every person is going to die[37] and we will each be held accountable for our thoughts, actions, and intentions- God is going to judge us.[38] People say things like, "Well, my god is not judgmental. My god will not judge me." In one sense, they are right. Their god will not judge them, because their "god" doesn't really exist. People often create gods in their own minds- gods that seem suitable to them,[39] but the truth is, people will not stand before the gods of their imaginations.

Everyone will stand before the True and Living God and will be held accountable for how they lived their life. Every thought, intention of your heart and every action will be judged by God. And the Bible tells us that "all have sinned and fall short of the glory of God"[40] and that "there is none righteous, no, not one."[41] People say, "Nobody is perfect."

---

[35] If you think I'm just trying to sell books, but you are interested in reading it, I'll gladly send you a copy for free.
[36] Hebrews 9:27
[37] Unless we get raptured. More about that in the next chapter
[38] If you have received Jesus as your Lord and Savior, your sins have already been judged on the cross.
[39] Romans 1:18-25
[40] Romans 3:23
[41] Romans 3:10

That's true, but it is also a dramatic understatement. We all fall far, far short of being anywhere close to "perfect."

Jesus said to the people of His day, "You have heard that it was said to those of old, 'You shall not murder, and whoever murders will be in danger of the judgment.' But I say to you that whoever is angry with his brother without a cause shall be in danger of the judgment."[42] Have you ever been angry at someone without a perfectly good reason? I sure have. If you are driving down the road and someone cuts in front of your car and you think, "Ugh, I could kill that guy!" You just killed him in your heart. How many murders does a person need to commit in order to be a murderer? One.

All the lies you have told in your life prove that you are a liar. If you have ever stolen anything, you are a thief. Do murderers, liars and thieves deserve to go to Heaven for eternity? No, we don't. In fact, the Bible tells us that "all liars" deserve to be in the lake of fire.[43] I could continue going through the 10 Commandments, but this should be enough for you to see that you have definitely "sinned"- you (and I) fall short of true and absolute goodness. And sin separates us from God.[44] "All we like sheep have gone astray."[45] God is absolutely righteous and Holy. He will not dwell in the presence of sin.[46]

Would a "good" judge allow murderers, liars and thieves- to go unpunished? No. If someone murdered your mother and your sister, would you be happy with a judge who issued a judgment for the murderer, "Oh, well, what's a murder or two? No problem. You can go free. Try not to do that too many more times." No, you would rightly be very upset with a judge like that. Their

---

[42] Matthew 5:21-22
[43] Revelation 21:8
[44] Isaiah 59:2
[45] Isaiah 53:6
[46] Psalm 5:4

judgment would not be true justice. And God is an absolutely just judge. In regard to our guilt, that's the bad news.

The Good News

But the Good News is that even though God is absolutely just and will judge sin; because God is love, He is also merciful. He made a way for us to be forgiven of our sins. Jesus said, "I am the way, the truth, and the life. No one comes to the Father except through Me."[47]

"For God so loved the world that He gave His only begotten Son, that whoever believes in Him should not perish but have everlasting life."[48]

Jesus, the Son of God, who existed with God in Heaven, came to this earth, lived a perfectly sinless life and then suffered and died on the cross to pay the penalty for your sins and mine. Then He rose again from the dead, just like the prophets predicted He would.[49] Jesus conquered death.[50]

The Bible says, "For the wages of sin is death, but the gift of God is eternal life in Christ Jesus our Lord."[51] The death that the Bible is talking about is an eternal separation from God. To reject God's gift of forgiveness is to choose to spend eternity in a place of torment- separated from all that is good and wonderful- separated from God and Heaven in a place the Bible describes as "the lake of fire."[52]

And no matter what sins you have committed, God does not want you to go there. We are clearly told that God is "not willing that any should perish but that all should come to repentance."[53] Repentance simply means to change your mind.

---

[47] John 14:6
[48] John 3:16
[49] Psalm 16:8-10; Psalm 22; Isaiah 53; Mark 8:31
[50] Revelation 1:18
[51] Romans 3:23
[52] Revelation 20:15
[53] 2 Peter 3:9

All you need to do to be forgiven of all your sins is to change your mind- turn to Jesus- decide to put your trust in Him as your Lord and Savior. Believe that He died on the cross for your sins and rose again on the third day. As the Bible says, "But as many as received Him, to them He gave the right to become children of God, to those who believe in His name"[54] And "if you confess with your mouth the Lord Jesus and believe in your heart that God has raised Him from the dead, you will be saved."[55]

You can be saved from the judgment you deserve. Pray to God. Ask Jesus to forgive your sins and to be your Lord and Savior- put your trust in Him and what He did for you on the cross.

The Gospel (the "good news") message is very simple. Jesus "died for our sins according to the Scriptures... He was buried, and He rose again the third day according to the Scriptures."[56] Decide to put your trust in Jesus- now.

If you have put your trust in Jesus- Congratulations! You have made the best and most important decision of your life- a decision that will change your eternal destiny. Becoming a follower of Jesus is not the same as joining a church or a religion. Being a follower of Jesus means you now have a personal relationship with God.

What's Next?

You might ask, "What's next?" If you are asking what the next step is as someone who has decided to trust in Jesus, turn to the "What's the next step as a new follower of Jesus?" on page 178. Then come back here and read the rest of this book. As for "What's next?" in the future, this next chapter will lay out the future according to what the God who is never wrong- tells us in the Bible.

---

[54] John 1:12
[55] Romans 10:9
[56] 1 Corinthians 15:3-4

10

"They're Gone!" The Rapture

"I go to prepare a place for you. And if I go and prepare a place for you, I will come again and receive you to Myself; that where I am, there you may be also."

- Jesus, in John 14:2-3

Depending on when you are reading this book, the sudden "catching away" (also known as the "rapture") of hundreds of millions of "born-again" Christians may have already taken place. If that is the case, all is not lost, but you will have some very difficult times ahead, as we will explain shortly. And the information we will lay out is very, very important for you to know. Whether it's already happened before you read this or not, it's important to know what it's all about.

The Rapture- What You Need to Know

First, let's look at the setting of the rapture- God's timeline of some of the "last days" world events. Before Jesus died, He told His followers, "... I will build My church ..."[1] So, Jesus' "church" didn't exist at the time. He spoke of it as being a future endeavor, saying He would build it. The word "church" in the Bible (in the original language) means "called out ones" and could be used to describe the "assembly" of those who are trusting in Jesus as their Lord and Savior. We are also told that the church is "His body"[2] and that we as

---

[1] Matthew 6:18
[2] Ephesians 1:22

followers of Jesus are compared to members of a body (like arms and legs, etc.) and Jesus is "the head" of the body.[3] When we personally receive Jesus into our lives, we each become joined spiritually to one another and to Jesus- as members of His body- His church.[4] So, when the Bible talks about the church, it is not talking about a building- it is talking about all the followers of Jesus. In the beginning of the New Testament book of Acts, God poured out His Spirit and the church was born.[5]

The Bible also predicts a time when the church will be "caught up" in the clouds to be with Jesus. And the Bible says we will be with Him forever. There are a number of world events that the Bible predicts will happen in the "last days." How many of them need to happen before the "catching away," the rapture of the church? Zero. The rapture could happen at any moment. In fact, if you read through the New Testament (written after Jesus went to Heaven), you will see that even early followers of Jesus were "eagerly waiting" for Jesus to come from Heaven.[6]

Jesus promised His followers, "In My Father's house are many mansions; if it were not so, I would have told you. I go to prepare a place for you. And if I go and prepare a place for you, I will come again and receive you to Myself; that where I am, there you may be also."[7] When Jesus left the earth, He rose up into Heaven.[8] That's where He is now,[9] and He said there are many "mansions" (which could be translated as "dwelling places") in Heaven. So, Jesus is in Heaven and promised His followers that He would come again and receive His followers to Himself, that where He is (in Heaven) we will be also. What will the "catching away" be like? It will be

---

[3] Colossians 1:18; 1 Corinthians 12-30
[4] 1 Corinthians 12-30
[5] Acts Chapter 2; See also Acts 11:15
[6] 1 Corinthians 1:7; 1 Thessalonians 1:10, 4:13-18
[7] John 14:2-3
[8] Luke 2:51
[9] 1 Peter 3:22

awesome. The amazing event is explained in several places in the New Testament.[10]

It is God's desire that every follower of Jesus would be "eagerly waiting" for Jesus to come to get us and take us to Heaven. Paul the Apostle, complimented some Christians because they "turned to God ... to serve the living and true God, and to wait for His Son from Heaven."[11]

What is the Rapture?

The Bible tells us, "For the Lord Himself will descend from heaven with a shout, with the voice of an archangel, and with the trumpet of God. And the dead in Christ will rise first. Then we who are alive and remain shall be caught up together with them in the clouds to meet the Lord in the air. And thus we shall always be with the Lord."[12]

The "dead in Christ" is referring to followers of Jesus who have died. Their souls are in Heaven with Jesus but their bodies "sleep"- they lie in the ground (or in the ocean, etc.) until Jesus comes in the clouds from Heaven "with a shout, with the voice of an archangel, and with the trumpet of God." The bodies of all the Christians who have died will rise up to join their souls, and we are told "we shall all be changed - in a moment, in the twinkling of an eye, at the last trumpet. For the trumpet will sound, and the dead will be raised incorruptible, and we shall be changed. For this corruptible must put on incorruption, and this mortal must put on immortality."[13]

When a seed is planted in the ground, it undergoes a transformation and grows up as a plant or a tree. In a similar way, when a follower of Jesus dies, their body (whether they are cremated or not) is in the ground (or ocean, etc.) but at the rapture, it will be raised up and instantly changed into a

---

[10] John 14:2-3; 1 Corinthian 15:51-55; 1 Thessalonians 4:13-17
[11] 1 Thessalonians 1:9-10
[12] 1 Thessalonians 4:16-17
[13] 1 Corinthians 15:51-53

wonderful spiritual body. It will be "immortal"- we will live forever (and never get sick, etc.).

And we are told, "Then we who are alive and remain shall be caught up together with them in the clouds to meet the Lord in the air. And thus we shall always be with the Lord."[14] The Christians who are living on the earth when Jesus comes from Heaven to get us, will be "caught up" together with the Christians who died before us. And we will all "meet the Lord in the air."

As followers of Jesus, we are "members of His body."[15] Jesus is "the head of the body,"[16] and it seems fitting that just as Jesus was raptured ("caught up") to Heaven,[17] that we as His followers, the body of Christ, will be raptured as well.

Is "the Rapture" Even Mentioned in the Bible?

Some well-meaning but ill-informed people will challenge Christians about the rapture, saying, "The word 'rapture' is not even in the Bible!" The truth is that no English word was in the original manuscripts of the Bible. The original manuscripts were written in Hebrew, Greek and Aramaic. The Greek word translated as "caught up" (or "caught away" in some Bibles) is the word "harpazo." When the Bible was translated into Latin, the Greek word "harpazo" was translated as the Latin word "rapiemur,"[18] which means "to seize, to carry off." That's where we get our English word "rapture."

The word (harpazo) is used 13 times in the New Testament and is translated in our English Bibles in slightly different ways in different verses, as "caught up,"[19] "caught

---

[14] 1 Thessalonians 4:17
[15] Ephesians 5:30
[16] Colossians 1:18
[17] Revelation 12:5
[18] www.blueletterbible.org/verse/vul/1th/4/17
[19] 2 Corinthians 12:2, 4; 1 Thessalonians 4:17; Revelation 12:5

away,"[20] "to take by force,"[21] "take,"[22] "catch,"[23] "snatch (pluck- KJV),"[24] "snatch away,"[25] and "pull."[26]

If someone mentions to you that the word "rapture" is not in the Bible, you might want to gently tell them that the word "Bible" is not in the Bible either, but it doesn't mean the Bible doesn't exist.

A Rose by Any Other Name Still Smells the Same

And the rapture by any other name still looks the same. Whether someone calls it the rapture, or whether they call it being caught up, caught away, taken by force, plucked, snatched, snatched away, grabbed or pulled; the idea is the same. The Bible teaches that Jesus will come in the air- in the clouds, and that all Christians who have died and those who are alive at the time of Jesus' arrival, will be caught up to be with Him, and He will take us to Heaven (where He has prepared a place for us)[27] and we will be with Him forever.

This is an absolutely amazing claim. Hundreds of millions of Christians all disappearing in an instant? Wow. The event will cause effects that will be felt all across the globe, and it will probably result in chaos in some places. Planes will suddenly be without pilots, cars without drivers, people will be fighting for Christians' property, etc. But life in Heaven is vastly better than life on earth, so all of us raptured Christians will be in absolute happiness. As the psalmist tells us, "In Your presence is fullness of joy; at Your right hand are pleasures forevermore."[28] Being in Heaven will be far better than anything we can even imagine.

---

[20] Acts 8:39
[21] Matthew 11:12, Acts 23:10
[22] John 6:15
[23] John 10:12
[24] John 10:28, 29
[25] Matthew 13:19
[26] Jude 1:23
[27] John 14:2-3
[28] Psalm 16:11

Heaven is not a state of mind. Jesus said, "I go to prepare a place for you. And if I go and prepare a place for you, I will come again and receive you to Myself; that where I am, there you may be also."[29] Heaven is a real place.

A Place Like No Other

We don't know exactly what eternity in Heaven will be like, but the Bible gives some descriptions that give us an idea. The Bible says, "And God will wipe away every tear from their eyes; there shall be no more death, nor sorrow, nor crying. There shall be no more pain, for the former things have passed away."[30] There are many, many wonderful things about Heaven. For one thing, Heaven is a place of absolute comfort. We may experience a lot of emotional pain in this life. Sometimes we are healed from the pain we suffer. Sometimes we may be hurt deeply and may not experience a complete healing in this life- but we will be completely healed in Heaven. We may have regrets about things we've done (or not done) in this life. In Heaven, we will be comforted.[31]

Will there be crying in Heaven? If there is, it will only be for a moment. You might say, "We'll leave our tears at the door." Every tear that we cry for anything will be wiped away by God Himself.[32] An angel won't wipe away our tears- God will. We won't walk through a machine with an automatic tear wiper. And God won't just wipe away some of our tears- He will wipe away every tear. What could we be sad about? Maybe we'll be grieving from things we have suffered on the earth. He will wipe away every tear. Maybe we will be sorry that we didn't live a life that was worthy of Him. Maybe we'll be grieving about people who didn't make it to Heaven. It doesn't matter what the source of our sorrow may be- He will

---

[29] John 14:2-3
[30] Revelation 21:4
[31] Luke 16:25
[32] Revelation 7:17

wipe away every tear. And then there will be no sorrow.[33] He is the "God of all comfort."[34] Isn't that awesome? You will have no sadness about anything- ever again. In Heaven, God Himself will comfort you with absolutely perfect comfort.

There will be no pain in Heaven.[35] I can't wait. I sometimes joke when people ask me if I have any allergies. I say, "Yes, I'm allergic to pain." I am looking forward to being in that place where there is absolutely no pain.

Some of us suffer in this life from chronic illnesses. In Heaven, we will be healed.[36] There will be no sickness.[37] Isn't that great? There will be no heart disease, no Cancer, strokes, diabetes, arthritis, Alzheimer's disease or Dementia; no colds or flu, no pneumonia or coughs, no sore backs or achy joints, no cuts or bruises or car accidents ... and there will be no doctors' offices or hospitals.

There will be no death.[38] That means we will not be getting old or decaying. We won't get wrinkles or age spots. Nobody will have dentures or crutches or wheelchairs or glasses. That is one of the wonderful things about Heaven- we'll never get old. We will live forever in a place that is so awesome- that we can't even imagine it! As the Bible says, "Eye has not seen, nor ear heard, nor have entered into the heart of man the things which God has prepared for those who love Him."[39] And there will be no taxes!

It all sounds so good. It's hard to imagine being free from all pain, sickness, sorrow, suffering and death. Does it sound too good to be true? It's no wonder that right after telling us

---

[33] Revelation 21:4
[34] 2 Corinthians 1:3
[35] Revelation 21:4
[36] Revelation 22:2
[37] Isaiah 33:24
[38] Revelation 21:4
[39] 1 Corinthians 2:9

about it, God reassures us by inserting a verse saying, "Write, for these words are true and faithful."[40]

All around us, we see things getting older and falling apart. Of course, it's not just our bodies that get old. Beautiful new cars get old, break down, rust and eventually end up in junk yards. Clothes wear out and end up in the trash. Houses wear out. Everything around us is getting older. Astronomers tell us that the entire universe is getting older and wearing out. It's suffering a slow death from heat loss. It's falling apart. Even the stars in the sky won't last forever- they're getting older. In fact, "the heavens" (the sky) and the earth will be destroyed by fire and God will make a new heaven (sky[41]) and earth.[42] The new earth and sky will never wear out. They will last forever.

In order not to devote too much space to this topic, I will simply add that Heaven will be a place of ultimate security and incredible beauty, and the greatest thing of all will be that we will be in the presence of the God of all glory, splendor and majesty, who created the universe and who loves us so much, that He was willing to send His Son from Heaven to come to the earth, to die on the cross to pay the penalty that our sins deserve.

Why Will God Rapture Believers?

God blesses those who love Him. Does He allow us to go through suffering? Yes (as explained in Chapter 14), but in the Bible, we also see that God demonstrates a clear pattern of rescuing His people <u>before</u> He pours out His judgment on sin- His "wrath." And regarding the coming time of the wrath of God being poured out on the earth (during the 7-year

---

[40] Revelation 21:5
[41] The same Greek word is used in the Bible for Heaven and for the sky (the "heavens") although they are two different things. The context of the verses makes clear which meaning is intended.
[42] 2 Peter 3:7-13

Tribulation),[43] the Bible clearly tells us that for all of us who trust in Christ- "God did not appoint us to wrath, but to obtain salvation through our Lord Jesus Christ."[44] We will be saved- rescued before the judgment of God is poured out.

The Bible tells us about Enoch, a man who had a close relationship with God- "And Enoch walked with God; and he was not, for God took him."[45] This "carrying away" of Enoch happened before the flood of Noah's day. In a similar way, God will "carry away" all of those who are trusting in Jesus as their Lord and Savior, before God brings a time of judgment on the earth.[46] You might wonder why God would send a flood to wipe out almost everyone on earth. We are told that in Noah's day, "the wickedness of man was great in the earth, and that every intent of the thoughts of his heart was only evil continually... and the earth was filled with violence... for all flesh had corrupted their way on the earth."[47]

While many people, including many scientists don't believe the entire earth was ever flooded by water (and I also used to believe the flood of Noah's day was a fairy tale), it is interesting to note that many scientists (including geologists, etc.) now believe there is strong evidence for a worldwide flood[48] and there are more than 270 different cultures around the world that have ancient stories about a worldwide flood.[49]

In speaking about the last days, Jesus told us, "... as it was in the days of Noah, so it will be also in the days of the Son of Man: They ate, they drank, they married wives, they were

---

[43] Deut. 4:26-32; Isa. 13:6-13; 17:4-11; Jer. 30:4-11; Ezek. 20:33-38; Dan. 9:27; 12:1; Zech. 14:1-4; Matt. 24:9-31. This period is graphically portrayed in Revelation 6–18, "the great Tribulation," 7:14; and "the hour of His judgment," 14:7.
[44] 1 Thessalonians 5:9
[45] Genesis 5:24
[46] Other theories of the timing of the rapture are discussed in Appendix 1 & 2 at the end of the book.
[47] Genesis 6:5, 11-12
[48] answersingenesis.org/the-flood/global/evidences-genesis-flood
[49] answersingenesis.org/the-flood/flood-legends/flood-legends

given in marriage, until the day that Noah entered the ark, and the flood came and destroyed them all. Likewise as it was also in the days of Lot: They ate, they drank, they bought, they sold, they planted, they built; but on the day that Lot went out of Sodom it rained fire and brimstone from heaven and destroyed them all."[50]

In Noah's day (about 2348 BC), God judged the people on earth with water. A few hundred years later, in Lot's day, God judged the cities of Sodom and Gomorrah with fire.[51] The Bible tells us that like in the days of Noah, in Lot's day the wickedness of Sodom and Gomorrah was terrible as well.[52]

Jesus points out some very significant things about the days of Noah (right before the flood) and the days of Lot (right before the destruction of Sodom and Gomorrah). For one thing, nothing seemed to be out of the ordinary. People were getting married and conducting business and farming. Other than the people who God had called away- nobody saw it coming. It will be the same when the rapture happens. The rapture will happen suddenly; and very soon afterwards, without warning, the 7-year Tribulation period will begin.

The 7-Year Tribulation

In Chapter 12 of this book, we will look more into what the 7-year Tribulation period consists of, but it is a time of God's wrath being poured out on the earth, as a judgment against those who are rebelling against God.[53] He will use the time of judgment to help many to see their need for forgiveness, and the terrible time on the earth will also be a time of many people turning to God and receiving the free gift of eternal life in Heaven.

---

[50] Luke 17:26-29
[51] answersingenesis.org/archaeology/have-we-found-sodom
[52] Genesis 18:20
[53] Deut. 4:26-32; Isa. 13:6-13; 17:4-11; Jer. 30:4-11; Ezek. 20:33-38; Dan. 9:27; 12:1; Zech. 14:1-4; Matt. 24:9-31. This period is graphically portrayed in Revelation 6–18 (cf. "the great Tribulation," 7:14; and "the hour of His judgment," 14:7)

Jesus said His return to the earth would be like "the days of Noah" and "the days of Lot." What did Jesus point out to us about those two times of judgment? First, in both Noah's day and Lot's day, things were going relatively smoothly and all of a sudden; judgment came.

Secondly, Jesus points out that the judgment of God was poured out on the earth after Noah went into the ark, and in Lot's day, the judgment of God was poured out "on the day that Lot went out of Sodom." Jesus' mention of the timing of the departure of Noah and Lot and the following judgments is significant. Jesus mentioned the timing (physical separation before judgment) in both instances. Why? Everything in the Bible is there for a reason.

The Timing of the Rapture

There are many followers of Jesus who believe that Christians will be raptured before the 7-year Tribulation period. But many other Christians believe the rapture will happen during (maybe in the middle of) the Tribulation and others believe the rapture will happen at the end of the Tribulation- when Jesus returns to the earth. This is not an issue to divide over as Christians. We should love each other and not have division over an issue like this.[54]

But the fact that many last days prophecies are being fulfilled in our lifetime means that what we believe about the timing of the rapture can make a big difference in how we live our lives. Are we "eagerly waiting" for Jesus to rapture us, or should we be expecting 3½ or 7 years of God's wrath on the earth first?

---

[54] An excellent book on the subject- *The Rapture Question,* by John Walvoord

Many believe that Jesus mentioned the "physical separation before judgment" examples of both Noah and Lot for a very good reason. He wants us to know that those who are trusting in Jesus will be rescued/separated like Noah and Lot were- before the time of judgment- not during or afterwards. In Noah's situation- "Then the LORD said to Noah, 'Come into the ark ...'"[55] God called Noah to Himself "and the Lord shut him in."[56] The LORD called Noah to come into the ark and shut him in the ark before the wrath of God was poured out on the earth (not in the middle, or after the wrath of God was poured out).

> "Then the LORD said to Noah, 'Come into the ark ...'" God called Noah to Himself "and the Lord shut him in." The LORD called Noah to come into the ark and shut him in the ark before the wrath of God was poured out on the earth.

Life on earth was going along as usual "until the day that Noah entered the ark, and the flood came and destroyed them all."[57] Notice that Jesus used the word "until." He specifically mentioned the timing of the events. The flood came after Noah and his family were already called into the ark to be with God, and were sealed inside, with the door closed- after "the Lord shut him in."[58]

In Lot's day, an angel of the Lord took hold of Lot's hand (along with his family) "and they brought him out and set him outside the city."[59] In fact, the angel of the Lord said to Lot, regarding the pouring out of the wrath of God on Sodom, and regarding the city to which Lot was going, "I cannot do anything until you arrive there." In other words, the angel was not allowed to pour out the wrath of God on Sodom until after

---

[55] Genesis 7:1
[56] Genesis 7:16
[57] Luke 17:27
[58] Genesis 7:16
[59] Genesis 19:16

Lot and his family left Sodom and had arrived safely in their new city.

This is very different than a situation in which Lot and his family were sitting in Sodom while the fire and brimstone rained down around them. And Noah and his family were not on the earth while the wrath of God was being poured out around them, either. No. Jesus made it very clear- in both Noah's and Lot's situations, that is not at all what happened. Jesus pointed out that both Noah's and Lot's families were physically separated before judgment came. Jesus used those two examples to describe the last days, and in both examples, Jesus points out the same timing- complete physical separation before judgment.

In the same way, many believe that first, Jesus "will descend from heaven with a shout," then we will be "caught up... to meet the Lord in the air."[60] And we believe that <u>after</u> we are safely in Heaven with Jesus, the wrath of God will be poured out in the Tribulation.

It also seems noteworthy that the order of events that Jesus mentions regarding Noah and Lot (separation before wrath) is the same order that the events are laid out in the Bible where it tells us about the rapture and the Tribulation. In the book of 1 Thessalonians, we are told about the rapture in the fourth chapter, and then in the fifth chapter, we are told about God's wrath being poured out in the Tribulation ("the day of the Lord"). We are told, "... when they say, 'Peace and safety!' then sudden destruction comes upon them, as labor pains upon a pregnant woman. And they shall not escape."[61] (For more information about the timing of the rapture, see Appendix 1 at the end of this book.)

---

[60] 1 Thessalonians 4:16-17
[61] 1 Thessalonians 5:3

In Case You Missed It

If you are reading this book after the rapture has taken place, rest assured, if you have put your trust in Jesus as your Lord and Savior (or if you do it right now), you will get to go to Heaven. You will have some extremely difficult times before going to Heaven (possibly including your execution), but you'll still get there.

What Happens Next?

There are a number of events that the Bible tells us will take place relatively soon. A couple of them could even happen before the rapture. We will look at those events in the next chapter, but the most significant events that will happen almost immediately after the rapture are going to change life on earth so radically that they really will lead to the end of the world as we know it. Everything from that point on will be different.

People on the earth will hardly be able to recognize the place. There used to be a game show on TV called, "Let's Make a Deal." Contestants were presented with choices. They could often choose "Door number 1, door number 2, or door number 3." There would be very different things behind each door. Some of them were great and some of them were not great at all. We are not in a TV game show, but when it comes to "getting right with God," people who choose to do it before the rapture will be eternally glad they did. Those who delay, will face a very, very rocky road. To delay and in effect, to choose "door number 2" will result in a very steep price being paid. And for many, they will pay the price forever.

Let's look at some soon-coming world events. After all, if you are driving down a road at night and there is a bridge out ahead, wouldn't you want there to be someone on the side of the road with a flashlight, warning you about the road ahead?

11

The New World Order

"They may talk of a 'new order' in the world, but what they have in mind is only a revival of the oldest and the worst tyranny."
— US President Franklin Roosevelt

The New World Order- Global Governance

In 1940, US President Franklin Roosevelt warned of a possible negotiated peace with Nazi Germany, "They may talk of a 'new order' in the world, but what they have in mind is only a revival of the oldest and the worst tyranny. In that there is no liberty, no religion, no hope. The proposed 'new order' is the very opposite of a United States of Europe or a United States of Asia. It is not a Government based upon the consent of the governed. It is not a union of ordinary, self-respecting men and women to protect themselves and their freedom and their dignity from oppression. It is an unholy alliance of power and pelf [stolen money] to dominate and enslave the human race."[1]

Many people around the world are currently working to bring about lasting world peace and economic security and prosperity for all- through global cooperation. Should we be opposed to that goal? Why wouldn't morally upright people across the globe support such efforts?

In an address to a joint session of Congress on September 11th, 1990, US President George H.W. Bush stated, "The crisis in the Persian Gulf, as grave as it is, also offers a rare

---

[1] Fireside Chat: The Arsenal of Democracy (December 29th 1940) : Roosevelt, Franklin D.

opportunity to move toward an historic period of cooperation. Out of these troubled times, our fifth objective - a new world order - can emerge: a new era, freer from the threat of terror, stronger in the pursuit of justice, and more secure in the quest for peace. An era in which the nations of the world, east and west, north and south, can prosper and live in harmony."

That was during the Persian Gulf War. A coalition of 40 nations, headed by the US, set out to liberate the country of Kuwait from the invasion by Iraq. Out of the chaos, the "troubled times" of the conflict, President Bush saw "a rare opportunity to move toward a historic period of cooperation... a new world order."

Adolph Hitler also had a vision to create a new world order- but his goal was global domination. In spite of what Hitler convinced many people of, his vision wasn't a good one and it didn't end well for him. The Bible predicts two (what might be called) "new world orders" in the last days. And these two "world orders" will have very different leaderships and very different futures. And as we saw with people who boarded the Titanic, when boarding a ship, having confidence is one thing, but knowing the truth about where you are heading is far more important.

The Bible tells us that one of the coming "world orders" will be ruled by Jesus Christ.[2] This one-world global government will be set up by Jesus Himself when He comes back to the earth and sets up His rule. When Jesus sets up His Kingdom on the earth, there will be no wars.[3] It will be a time when peace truly prevails on the earth. It will be a wonderful time to be alive. (We'll look more at this shortly.)

But the Bible also predicts that shortly before the wonderful global government ruled by Jesus Christ, there will be another new world order. This global government will

---

[2] Zechariah 14:9
[3] Isaiah 2:4

initially be ruled by a group of ten leaders.[4] There are quite a few great books that delve into everything the Bible teaches about the "last days" one-world government, but due to the fact that we don't want this book to be too long, we will just look at certain aspects of this coming "new world order."

Order Out of Chaos

When there is chaos, it makes sense that people would want to work to bring order- peace, cooperation and security. Those are noble goals. For many years "conspiracy theorists" have claimed that there are groups of people (whose memberships have changed over time) who intentionally create or contribute to chaos in different areas of the world, in order to be able to swoop in as the heroes to save the day through the bringing about of their version of "order" (control).[5] Whether we agree with this claim or not, we, as people living in the last days, need to take Jesus' warning seriously- "Do not be deceived."

The results of being deceived could be personally and eternally catastrophic. If you are alive on the earth when the Antichrist sets up his kingdom (because you were not trusting in Christ, so you weren't taken up in the rapture) and you fall for the deception of the "peace making" Antichrist, you will pay the ultimate price. You do not want to board the wrong ship- especially a ship heading for a destination with eternal consequences.

The Bible tells us there will be two "saviors" in the future. One is the Antichrist, who will be somewhat of a counterfeit Christ- a false Christ who is opposed to the real Christ. He will be a "peace maker"[6] who knows how to "say all the right things" but will deceive the world into following him.

---

[4] Daniel 2; 7:24; Revelation 17:12
[5] For further reading- *Spirit of the Antichrist* Vol. 1 & 2, & *Spirit of the False Prophet*, by J.B. Hixson.
[6] Daniel 9:27

He will be very persuasive and very deceptive. He will come on the scene "with all power, signs, and lying wonders, and with all unrighteous deception ..."[7] He will be a miracle worker, and it will be very easy for people to want to believe his lies. "He shall prosper and thrive... Through his cunning, he shall cause deceit to prosper under his rule."[8]

At first, he may say things like, "It doesn't matter what you believe, as long as you are sincere and your thoughts lead toward peace. All roads lead to God. In fact, you are God." Or he may not mention religion at all. But in time, his rule will become much more severe and authoritarian. For example, as we looked at earlier, people will not be allowed to buy or sell without taking his mark on their right hand or forehead. (But of course, the mark will probably be hailed as being necessary for world peace, security and prosperity.) This false Christ will rise from obscurity to power during the 7-year Tribulation period, when the ten world leaders hand their "power and authority" to him.[9] And "he shall destroy fearfully."[10]

Recognizing the Antichrist- the 7-Year Agreement

Through the years, many people have speculated about who the Antichrist ("the beast") may be. A charismatic leader comes along who seems to oppose Christians, Jews and the nation of Israel, and people add up the numerical equivalents of the letters of their name (in Greek or Hebrew) and they add up to 666. "Wow! This guy may be the Antichrist!" As of the writing of this book, we don't know who the Antichrist is. Is he alive on earth now? Very possibly, but at the time of the writing of this book, we simply don't know who he is. But people can know for sure once he steps into his place of power. How can people know?

---

[7] 2 Thessalonians 2:9-10
[8] Daniel 8:24-25
[9] Revelation 17:11-13; Daniel 2; 7:24
[10] Daniel 8:24

In the Old Testament book of Daniel, chapter nine, Daniel lays out some last days events. Without getting into too many details here, we'll simply say that Daniel tells us that the Messiah would be killed,[11] and of course, just as he predicted, Jesus, the Messiah was killed (crucified), that the Antichrist will "confirm" or "enforce" a seven year agreement with Israel (and the Antichrist may even help facilitate the rebuilding of the temple in Jerusalem), but in the middle of that seven year period (3½ years into the agreement), he will stop people from making sacrifices and offerings in the temple in Jerusalem.[12]

If you happen to be alive during this time period (due to your having missed the rapture), you can know exactly who the Antichrist is- he is the man who makes the 7-year peace agreement with Israel (maybe involving some Muslim nations) and who, 3½ years later, stops the temple sacrifices and goes in and sits in the temple- wanting to be worshipped as God.[13]

His false prophet frontman will order an "image of the beast"(a likeness of the Antichrist) to be created and as we will look at shortly, the "image" (AI robot?) of the Antichrist will be able to breathe and speak.[14] Paul the Apostle tells us, "... the man of sin is revealed, the son of perdition, who opposes and exalts himself above all that is called God or that is worshiped, so that he sits as God in the temple of God, showing himself that he is God."[15] So, the Antichrist will go into the temple and want to be worshipped as God, and the "abomination of desolation" will be set up in the temple[16] (probably the "image of the beast").

---

[11] Daniel 9:26
[12] Daniel 9:27
[13] Daniel 9:27; 2 Thessalonians 2:3-4
[14] Revelation 13:14-15
[15] 2 Thessalonians 2:3-4
[16] Matthew 24:15

A Miraculous Healing!

The Antichrist, "the lawless one," will also be healed of a deadly head wound he receives in an assassination attempt- and will lose sight in one eye and lose the use of one arm,[17] and people across the world will be amazed at his healing as well as the powerful military that he commands. he will get his authority from the devil himself (yes, there really is a devil)- "And I saw one of his heads as if it had been mortally wounded, and his deadly wound was healed. And all the world marveled and followed the beast. So they worshiped the dragon [the devil] who gave authority to the beast; and they worshiped the beast, saying, 'Who is like the beast? Who is able to make war with him?'"[18]

If you are alive on the earth at the time these events take place, and you know these few things- you can clearly identify the Antichrist. He will deceive a lot of people but will turn out to be the most evil human being who has ever lived.

The "Abomination of Desolation"

People around the world will be amazed by this man. he helps to secure world peace and prosperity; he is an incredibly persuasive speaker and is miraculously healed from a deadly head wound. he will come on the scene as someone who is not very impressive,[19] but in time he will astound people. And the people of Israel will marvel as well. Since (just as the Bible predicted) most of the Jewish people on earth don't realize that Jesus fulfilled the (hundreds of) Old Testament predictions regarding the Messiah,[20] many are still waiting for the "prince of peace"[21] to come on the scene. They don't realize that He's already been here once.

---

[17] Zechariah 11:17
[18] Revelation 13:3-4
[19] Daniel 8:9
[20] Isaiah 53:1, 3-4
[21] Isaiah 9:6

When the charismatic, miracle working Antichrist (along with his miracle working sidekick- the false prophet) comes on the scene and helps establish or enforce the peace agreement in the middle east that the Jews have long waited for, many people in Israel will think the Antichrist is actually the Messiah that they have been hoping for- or at least a "political Messiah." Jesus prophesied to the leaders of Israel in His day, "I have come in My Father's name, and you do not receive Me; if another comes in his own name, him you will receive."[22]

Jesus expands on the prophecy about the Antichrist and the temple in Jerusalem, telling us that when the Antichrist's image is set up in the temple, that is the signal to the Jews in Israel- to flee- "Therefore when you see the 'abomination of desolation,' spoken of by Daniel the prophet, standing in the holy place (whoever reads, let him understand), then let those who are in Judea flee to the mountains... For then there will be great Tribulation, such as has not been since the beginning of the world until this time, no, nor ever shall be."[23] When the Antichrist's image is set up, and the Jewish people realize that the Antichrist is not the Messianic world leader they had hoped he was, he will turn on the people of Israel and begin slaughtering them. That's why Jesus warns them to immediately flee to the mountains.

Paying a Price for Not Following the Antichrist

But as we looked at in Chapter 8, the Jewish people aren't the only ones the Antichrist will kill. Everyone who refuses to take "the mark of the beast" (the "666") on their right hand or forehead will be targets for the Antichrist and the false prophet. The book of Revelation, the last book in the Bible, lays out the timing of some of the events of the rule of the Antichrist.

---

[22] John 5:24
[23] Matthew 24:15-16, 21

In Revelation chapter 13, we are told: the Antichrist is given power and "great authority," empowered by the devil (vss. 1-2), the Antichrist is healed of his deadly head wound received from an attack (v. 3), people openly worship (revere or respect) the devil ("the dragon") and the Antichrist (v. 4), the false prophet performs miracles on behalf of the Antichrist, including calling fire down from heaven and through those "great signs," he deceives people on the earth (v. 13), the false prophet directs people to create an image of the Antichrist (that breathes) and causes it to speak (v. 14-15), the image of the Antichrist causes the death of anyone who will not worship (revere or respect) it (v. 15) and the false prophet orders everyone to receive the mark of the Antichrist (the beast). People will not be allowed to buy or sell without it (v. 16-17).

Anyone who refuses to bow down to the devil's representative on the earth, faces possible execution- "the image of the beast should both speak and cause as many as would not worship the image of the beast to be killed."[24] And needless to say, by not taking the mark, people will lose the ability to buy the basic necessities of life- food and clothing, etc. and won't be able to sell things. Death is the price people will pay for not submitting to the Antichrist and his one world government. And many people will pay this price.[25]

But the Bible clearly warns that the consequences for taking the mark of the beast- the consequences for following this satanic world leader and his world governmental system- are far worse than being executed.

Paying a Higher Price for Following the Antichrist

God clearly warns, "If anyone worships the beast and his image, and receives his mark on his forehead or on his hand, he himself shall also drink of the wine of the wrath of God, which is poured out full strength into the cup of His

---

[24] Revelation 13:15
[25] Revelation 7:9-14

indignation. He shall be tormented with fire and brimstone in the presence of the holy angels and in the presence of the Lamb. And the smoke of their torment ascends forever and ever; and they have no rest day or night, who worship the beast and his image, and whoever receives the mark of his name."[26] This Scripture really doesn't need any explanation. Anyone who bows down to this globalist system and its leaders - anyone who takes the mark - will suffer the wrath of God and will be sent to Hell for eternity.

Again, if you are alive on the earth during this period of time, whatever you do, DO NOT TAKE THE MARK! The price for refusing the mark may be starvation or execution (and if you have children, they may take them away from you), but the price for taking the mark will be separation from God and all that is good, in a place of torment- for eternity.

An Image that Breathes and Talks?

As John said in verse 15, "the image of the beast should both speak and cause as many as would not worship (revere or respect) the image of the beast to be killed." Two thousand years ago when that prophecy was made, it must have sounded crazy. An image (a likeness)- like a statue, will be able to breathe and talk?

But fast forward to today- with the development of artificial intelligence and even robots that can breathe; for the first time in human history, we live in a day when "an image" (a likeness)- possibly a robot, can be set up that breathes, speaks and even makes decisions.

It's reported that robots that "breathe" help people to relax when they are near them. That would be a nice touch for the "image of the beast." (Although the fact that the "image of the beast" will cause many people's deaths will no doubt take away some of the "relaxing" features of this dreadful creation.)

---

[26] Revelation 14:9-11

Two thousand years ago, this must have sounded ridiculous. Even 30 years ago, this would have sounded like something from a Sci-fi movie. But today, it's a very possible reality. There are now AI robots that can breathe, speak, make decisions and even cause actions to take place- even life-ending actions. As far back as 2007 in Iraq, the US military has been using robots in warfare. Robots are now being created that can end people's lives in a number of different ways, and militaries all over the world are developing deadly robots.

Of course, if the "image of the beast" is connected to a network such as Elon Musk's Starlink satellite network; with a little global government coordination, the "image of the beast" may be able to direct police actions all around the world- specifically- causing as many as will not respect the image of the beast or take the mark- to be killed.

Who Would Allow That?!

The natural response to a scenario like that might be, "Who in the world would allow such a thing?" Well, what if in order to "stop terrorism all around the world" or to "stop almost all crime worldwide, including human trafficking," a system of global digital identification (which is already being established), monitoring and obedience to a few simple rules and travel restrictions (maybe including 15-minute cities, etc.) would result in world peace and the elimination of almost all crime? Or what if it could "save the planet from extinction due to climate change"? Or (this may sound far-fetched) what if world leaders tell us there are extraterrestrials among us who mean us harm ("an invasion") and that a global digital ID implant system is "the only way to save us from the invasion," i.e.- the only way to distinguish us from them? Don't you think people around the world would be willing to obey the global government (and the "well meaning" business leaders) whose stated goals are world peace, security and prosperity? Just as world (political and business) leaders promoted the Covid-19 injections- "If you care about others, you'll take the shot," the same logic may be used- "If you care about others, you'll take the mark. How can you be so selfish as to not take the mark?"

"Just take a little mark (an implant or smart tattoo, etc.) on your right hand or forehead, and you'll be allowed to buy and sell." Without it? "No Mark - No Sale!" Imagine the ramifications of not being able to buy or sell. People will get very hungry - very quickly. But if you "just respect the directions from the new and wonderful world leader who has everyone's best interest at heart, you'll do just fine." Oh, and at some point, people will probably need to stop going to church- at least Bible-believing Christian churches- especially churches that teach about Bible prophecy.

A sad sidenote on this point- the Bible warns that "... in latter times some will depart from the faith, giving heed to deceiving spirits and doctrines of demons."[27] Not only are many televangelists actually just money-grubbing "wolves in sheep's clothing"[28] - false teachers and false prophets, but there is also a growing movement among Christian churches called the New Apostolic Reformation (NAR).

Millions of American Christians don't even know they are caught up in this last days deception. One of their numerous false beliefs is that God is raising up apostles and prophets to take over leadership of churches all over the earth,[29] and that through the "Seven Mountain Mandate"- they will establish God's Kingdom on earth by taking control over the areas of family, religion, education, media, arts/entertainment, business, and government before Jesus returns.

Completely contrary to what the Bible teaches about the last days, their "miracle working" false prophets and false apostles expect to take dominion over the earth.

---

[27] 1 Peter 4:1
[28] Matthew 7:15
[29] See: www.gotquestions.org/New-Apostolic-Reformation.html and www.hollypivec.com and www.apologeticsindex.org/2977-new-apostolic-reformation-overview

Unfortunately, just as Jesus said about the last days, "Then many false prophets will rise up and deceive many."[30] This almost militant "Christian nationalist" movement will likely provide justification for many people who want to persecute Christians in the last days.

NAR's "mandate" is built on a dual misunderstanding of Scripture and of Christ's purposes in the world. Needless to say, correct teaching about last days Bible prophecy is completely foreign to them, and they will probably be quite shocked as the new world order continues to advance across the globe- in spite of all their "declaring" and "decreeing."

During the Tribulation, Bible teaching churches may be outlawed or silenced due to all of the supposed "hate speech" and "disinformation" that will be coming from people who believe the Bible. The global government will likely try to prevent people from sharing truth about the real Jesus, what the Bible reveals about the future- including the rapture, the new world order, the Antichrist and the mark of the beast, etc.

The prophet Daniel tells us about the Antichrist- "Then the king shall do according to his own will: he shall exalt and magnify himself above every god, shall speak blasphemies against the God of gods, and shall prosper till the wrath has been accomplished; for what has been determined shall be done."[31] The Antichrist will not be a friend of real Christians or Jews. In fact, he will kill them. So, if you are reading this book after the rapture has taken place, realize that if you have put your trust in Jesus as your Lord and Savior, you will go to Heaven for eternity, but in the meantime, you may be killed for your faith.

---

[30] Matthew 24:11. Some of the leaders typically associated with the NAR are C. Peter Wagner, Che Ahn, John and Carol Arnott, Heidi and Roland Baker, Mike Bickle, Bill Hamon, Stacey Campbell, Randy Clark, James Goll, Cindy Jacobs, Rick Joyner, Bill Johnson and Kris Vallotton of the Bethel Church, Patricia King, Chuck Pierce, Dutch and Tim Sheets, Brian Simmons (the Passion Translation) and "Apostle" Paula White-Cain.

[31] Daniel 11:36-37

12

The End of the World as We Know It

"I think you all know that I've always felt the nine most terrifying words in the English language are: 'I'm from the Government, and I'm here to help.'"
- President Ronald Reagan

The Leader of the New World Order

God gave John, an Apostle of Jesus, a vision in which he predicts this new world order (the final world empire before Jesus returns). In the vision, John saw a 10 headed beast, and the Bible interprets that vision for us. There will be 10 world leaders who will rule for a short time and then give their authority to one leader- "The ten horns which you saw are ten kings [leaders] who have received no kingdom as yet, but they receive authority for one hour [a short time] as kings with the beast. These are of one mind, and they will give their power and authority to the beast."[1] This "beast," the "Antichrist" will become very, very powerful. The Bible says, "And authority was given him over every tribe, tongue [language], and nation."[2] That's more authority than anyone in human history has ever had.

Do we want there to be world peace and cooperation? Of course. But would any of us want to be part of a new world order ruled by someone like Adolph Hitler? Of course not. The prophet Daniel tells us, "His power shall be mighty, but

---

[1] Revelation 17:12-13
[2] Revelation 13:7

not by his own power; he shall destroy fearfully, and shall prosper and thrive; he shall destroy the mighty, and also the holy people [the Jewish people in Israel]. Through his cunning he shall cause deceit to prosper under his rule;"[3]

We see from this prophecy that the Antichrist will be extremely powerful and authoritarian. He will be a man who is a destroyer- a man of destruction. And as we looked at in the last chapter- under his leadership- "deceit will prosper." It's no wonder that in laying out the future events of the last days, Jesus repeatedly warned us about deception. The disciples asked, "And what will be the sign of Your coming, and of the end of the age?" The first thing that Jesus said was, "Take heed that no one deceives you. For many will come in My name, saying, 'I am the Christ,' and will deceive many."[4] That's exactly what the Antichrist will do- he will deceive many- and may likely even claim to be "the Christ".

A One-Size Fits Most- Global Religion

While the evil new world order that President Roosevelt warned about in World War II was primarily military and political in nature, the new world order (that many believe is already spreading around the world) will be economic, political, military and will also be religious- at least at first. Revelation chapter 17 tells us about a global end times religious system that is in opposition to the True God. The false religious system will work together with the one-world government to gain power and influence over humanity, and will have a great amount of influence over "peoples, multitudes, nations, and tongues [languages],"[5] but once the globalists have the control they are seeking, they will have no further use for the global religious system and they will turn

---

[3] Daniel 8:24-25
[4] Matthew 24:4-5
[5] Revelation 17:15

on this spiritual "harlot" (prostitute) religion and destroy its power.[6]

There is an increasing movement around the world that seeks to bring world religions together. It's called "syncretism" (a merging of different religions) and is being moved forward under the guise of "ecumenicalism." The idea is that the most important thing is that we all get along. It sounds good enough to many- "Don't all religions basically teach the same things? Can't they all just be combined into one religion?" And that idea makes a lot of sense- unless truth matters. The truth is that while there are similarities between many of the world's religions, there are also numerous areas in which the religions of the world significantly contradict each other- so they cannot all be true.

For example, the Bible clearly teaches that Jesus is the Son of God.[7] The Quran of the Muslims teaches that, "Allah has not taken any son, nor has there ever been with Him any deity."[8] Contradictory statements of fact cannot both be true. And neither can self-contradicting statements. For example, if someone says, "It's true that there is no truth," or "A dog is not a dog," those are self-contradicting statements. (It cannot be true that "there is no truth.") And God either has a Son or He doesn't. The contradictory claims that, "Jesus is the Son of God," and "God has not taken any son," cannot both be true.

Yuval Harari, an advisor to the globalist World Economic Forum (WEF) speaking of artificial intelligence, stated, "AI can create new ideas. [It] can even write a new Bible... In a few years, there might be religions that are actually correct..."[9] Mr. Harari sounds like a great potential priest for the coming global harlot religion. Many people believe this

---

[6] Revelation 17:15-16
[7] John 1:1, 14
[8] The Noble Quran 23:91
[9] www.christianpost.com/news/israeli-futurist-predicts-ai-will-soon-write-a-new-bible.html

global religion is already being established through the efforts of organizations such as the World Council of Churches, whose stated goals include, "to develop interreligious solidarities..."[10]

As we move into the future and get closer to the rise of the Antichrist, we can expect to see the global (harlot) religion continuing to rise on the world stage.

And we should expect to see the "ten horns,"[11] the ten global leaders (although possibly completely behind the scenes) consolidating their control over global issues.

Who Are the Ten "Kings"?

The Bible doesn't tell us who they are, so we can't know for certain. And the Bible doesn't tell us whether at the time of the Antichrist's rise to power, the ten world leaders who are in power at the time (and may even be in power now), will be well-known to people. They may be government leaders (Presidents, Prime Ministers, etc.) or they may be rich and powerful business leaders or technocrats who have tremendous influence in the world- such as Bill Gates, Klaus Schwab, Yuval Harari, Elon Musk, Peter Thiel, Larry Ellison, George and Alex Soros, the Rockefellers, the Rothschilds, etc. They may even be people whose names we wouldn't even recognize. People who have studied the many "behind the scenes" power brokers in the world talk about secret societies and globalist groups such as the Freemasons, the World Economic Forum, the European Union, the Trilateral Commission, the Council on Foreign Relations, the Illuminati, the Rosicrucians, the Order of Skull and Bones, the Club of Rome, Bohemian Grove, the Bilderbergers, the Round Table Group, Knights Templar, Opus Dei and the United Nations, etc.[12]

---

[10] www.oikoumene.org/what-we-do/interreligious-dialogue-and-cooperation
[11] Revelation 17:12-13
[12] For more information, you might want to read books such as- Spirit of the Antichrist Vol. 1 & 2, & Spirit of the False Prophet, by J.B. Hixson

While the Bible doesn't specifically tell us who the ten leaders are (or will be), the Bible does seem to indicate that the central power of this last days' union will come out of an area that many Bible prophecy teachers call, "the revived Roman empire." More than 500 years before Christ, the prophet Daniel accurately told us of the succession of (at the time- future) major world empires.

World Empires

During Daniel's time, Nebuchadnezzar (the king of Babylon) had conquered the Jewish kingdom of Judah and Daniel was in his service. Nebuchadnezzar had a dream in which he saw a giant statue and each part of the statue represented a different kingdom. Daniel was able to tell the king what he had dreamed, as well as to give the interpretation of the dream, "You, O king, were watching; and behold, a great image!

"This great image, whose splendor was excellent, stood before you; and its form was awesome. This image's head was of fine gold, its chest and arms of silver, its belly and thighs of bronze, its legs of iron, its feet partly of iron and partly of clay.... And in the days of these kings the God of heaven will set up a kingdom which shall never be destroyed; and the kingdom shall not be left to other people; it shall break in pieces and consume all these kingdoms, and it shall stand forever. Inasmuch as you saw that the stone was cut out of the mountain without hands, and that it broke in pieces the iron, the bronze, the clay, the silver, and the gold – the great God has made known to the king what will come to pass after this. The dream is certain, and its interpretation is sure."[13]

And just as Daniel predicted- one after another- four great empires have risen since Daniel's day- Babylon, Medo-Persia (Iran), Greece, and Rome became world empires. Many people who study the Bible would say we are now in the midst of the establishment of a revived Roman empire- the fifth empire Daniel predicted. This will be the last of the world empires that exists before the return of Jesus Christ to the earth. Jesus ("the stone" in the dream) will crush all that remains of the former world empires and will set up His eternal Kingdom. Daniel tells us that while the ten leaders are still active, "in the days of these kings the God of heaven will set up a kingdom which shall never be destroyed." (That will be at Jesus' return to the earth.)

An interesting sidenote is that just as the metals mentioned in Daniel's vision become successively lower in value, they become harder in strength (gold, silver, bronze and iron)- just like each of the kingdoms mentioned. For example, the fourth kingdom- the Roman empire (which relied heavily upon iron) was militarily strong but not as wealthy as the earlier kingdoms.

The last (fifth) great kingdom to rule the world before the Lord returns to set up His Kingdom on earth is the revived Roman Empire (including some western European nations). Many Bible commentators say that it is being (or is already) set up. Notice that Daniel says of this kingdom, "its feet partly of iron and partly of clay." While iron is a lot harder than clay (so some elements of this kingdom may be like iron- stronger militarily and economically), other elements are more fragile (and weaker- like clay). And of course, we know that iron and clay don't mix well, so, we should expect that the "last days empire" will be a combination of powerful and not so

---

[13] Daniel 2:31-32, 44-45

powerful nations and that the bonds between these nations will probably not be very strong. As Daniel tells us, "And as you saw the feet and toes, partly of potter's clay and partly of iron, it shall be a divided kingdom."[14] It's interesting that some of the European Union nations are a lot stronger than others, and there is a lack of total unity among them- like there would be if you tried to mix iron with clay.

The deceptive Antichrist, "the beast," will at some point rise up and show his true (and ruthless) colors as he leads the final kingdom before Jesus returns. But then, as Daniel tells us, "And in the days of these kings the God of heaven will set up a kingdom which shall never be destroyed ... and it shall stand forever."[15] Jesus will return to the earth to set up His Kingdom- the truly wonderful new world order- and He will completely destroy the Antichrist and his kingdom.

Worldwide Deception

A significant part of the global government and the Antichrist's arrival on the scene is a massive, worldwide deception.[16] Paul the Apostle, tells us that there is a restraining force that will be "taken out of the way"[17] and that the Antichrist will be revealed and the massive deception will take place once that restrainer is removed.[18]

Many Bible scholars identify the restraining force- "He who restrains" as the Holy Spirit working in the lives of Christians. There is strong Biblical support for this position (which, for the sake of brevity, we won't explain here).

Once the rapture happens and the Christians are "taken out of the way,"[19] it will be a lot easier for the global government to take full control and for the Antichrist to rise

---

[14] Daneil 2:41
[15] Daniel 9:44
[16] 2 Thessalonians 2:10-12
[17] 2 Thessalonians 2:7-8
[18] 2 Thessalonians 2:7-12
[19] 2 Thessalonians 2:7

to power. If there were hundreds of millions of Bible believing Christians on the earth when a man came on the scene who had been "miraculously healed" after an assassination attempt (losing sight in one eye and the use of one arm[20]), who made (or enforced) a 7-year agreement with Israel, and the temple in Jerusalem was rebuilt or was in the process of being rebuilt, Christians all over the would be sounding the alarm- "He's the Antichrist! Watch out! Don't take the mark!" It would be far more difficult for this man to deceive the world's population if we pesky Christians were exposing him for who he is.

But once Christians who have some Bible knowledge are "taken out of the way,"[21] the path for the Antichrist will be smooth. He can waltz in and deceive the world with his miracles and "one-world peace and prosperity plan" (or whatever he may call it).

> Once Christians who have some Bible knowledge are "taken out of the way," the path for the Antichrist will be smooth. He will waltz in and deceive the world with his miracles and "one-world peace and prosperity plan."

Paul the Apostle tells us, "And then the lawless one will be revealed, whom the Lord will consume with the breath of His mouth and destroy with the brightness of His coming. The coming of the lawless one is according to the working of Satan, with all power, signs, and lying wonders, and with all unrighteous deception among those who perish, because they did not receive the love of the truth, that they might be saved. And for this reason, God will send them strong delusion, that they should believe the lie, that they all may be condemned who did not believe the truth but had pleasure in unrighteousness."[22]

When the Antichrist (the lawless one) comes on the scene with "power, signs, and lying wonders, and with all

---

[20] Zechariah 11:17
[21] 2 Thessalonians 2:7
[22] 2 Thessalonians 2:8-12

unrighteous deception," who will be deceived by him? "Those who perish, because they did not receive the love of the truth, that they might be saved."

God gives people the freedom to make choices. And when people refuse to accept the truth, God gives them over to the lies they love. People who reject the truth, "suppress the truth in unrighteousness,"[23] and because they would rather believe a lie than turn to the truth, "God will send them strong delusion, that they should believe the lie, that they all may be condemned who did not believe the truth but had pleasure in unrighteousness."[24]

What Deception?

You might wonder what type of mass deception people all over the world would fall for. At this point we can only guess, but based on the things being communicated in the mass (globalist stooge) media recently, it could be something involving extraterrestrials and/or signs in the sky.

"Extraterrestrials" are not actually alien life forms from distant galaxies, they are demonic beings.[25] As I mentioned earlier, before I received Jesus, I had several experiences with extraterrestrials (communicating with and seeing UFO's, etc.).[26] It is not important that you believe me about my experiences, but it's my personal opinion (and many others' opinion as well) that extraterrestrials may very well be part of the great deception that occurs after the rapture.[27]

It could be that the Antichrist and his ilk will use extraterrestrials as a way to explain the rapture- "Hundreds of millions of people were taken from the earth by

---

[23] Romans 1:18
[24] 2 Thessalonians 2:11-12
[25] For more information about the demonic nature of extraterrestrials, watch the video: Alien Intrusion. Info at: alienintrusion.com and/or check out- https://creation.com/en/topics/aliens
[26] As detailed in my book, A Different Life – The Strat Goodhue Story (available for free upon request).
[27] 2 Thessalonians 2:8-12

extraterrestrials! We need to unite as a world population to defend against these alien invaders!"

Or maybe the alien deception will sound something like this- "We are now in communication with extraterrestrials, who tell us that they have been in the universe for millions of years. They are far more evolved than we are, and they have informed us that humans were brought to the earth many years ago. There is no longer any need to believe in old-fashioned traditional religions. Christianity was just a crutch to help the human species, but people no longer need silly notions such as God and Jesus, etc. That's why the extraterrestrials did us all a favor by removing those narrow-minded Christians from the earth. They just weren't ready to adapt to humanity's next step of evolution."

Or the deception could be something harmless sounding, like, "If you take this little implant, you can download books, languages, a college education (etc.) into your brain in just minutes. And it contains a very convenient digital ID (making the world a much 'safer' place) and you'll be able to buy and sell, too!" Certainly, people wouldn't want to miss out on being able to download massive amounts of information into their brains in just a few minutes.

> **It very well could be that the Antichrist and his ilk will use extraterrestrials as a way to explain the rapture- "Hundreds of millions of people were taken from the earth by extraterrestrials! We need to unite!"**

Who wouldn't want to become "instantly brilliant" (like one of Elon Musk's Optimus robots)? Who would want to remain like their ignorant un-downloaded "cave man" neighbors? Of course, this sort of technology could easily open the door to behavior modification. If "what you know" can be put in your brain, then "how you think" can be as well. This would help explain why the Bible tells us that anyone who "receives the mark" will be eternally damned.[28] Once the mark is received- people's minds will be made up- their fate will be sealed.

It's just a thought, but at the current rate of the advancement of technology, the promise of "eternal life" may also be offered. All people would need to do, would be to receive the implant (with the mark) so their brains can be connected to robots and/or the internet. If people's bodies are not working well or start to wear out, people could (supposedly) "transfer" their minds to robots (their new bodies) or upload them to the cloud, and (in theory) live forever. The oldest lie in the Book- "You will not surely die,"[29] was spoken by the devil to Eve in the garden of Eden. And it may be a lie that is told to everyone on earth in the last days.

One last thought along these lines- when the Gog-Magog invasion takes place (the Russia, Iran, Turkey, Libya, etc. alliance invading Israel), the Antichrist may try to take credit for God's supernatural and miraculous intervention that will end that war (which will include a massive earthquake, flooding rain, great hailstones, fire, and burning balls of sulfur).[30] The Antichrist may claim that it was his own miracle working power that wiped out the invading armies, and he could use the false claim to solidify his power.

We don't know what form this deception will take but a guess is that whatever it is, it may include an appeal to people's emotions- like, "If you really care about people, you'll submit to the new world leader's plan."

I'll Just Wait Until After the Rapture

Many people who have heard about Jesus and the rapture, say things like, "Well, once the rapture happens, and millions of Christians disappear off the face of the earth, then I'll know you guys are right, and I'll become a Christian." There are several serious problems with this plan.

---

[28] Revelation 14:9-11
[29] Genesis 3:4
[30] Ezekiel 38:18-23

One problem is that "He who is often rebuked, and hardens his neck, will suddenly be destroyed, and that without remedy."[31] People who hear the truth and reject it, over time become more hardened against it. Hearing and rejecting the truth is a dangerous path to follow. The Bible says, "Behold, now is the accepted time; behold, now is the day of salvation."[32] If you are reading this book and have not yet turned to Jesus and put your trust in Him, what will it take? How much evidence is enough? Do you really believe that all of the fulfilled prophecies shared in this book (which are just a fraction of the hundreds and hundreds of fulfilled Biblical prophecies) are just coincidences? Really? Are you willing to risk your heart becoming harder and harder- to the point where you are "without remedy"?

Another problem with the "I'll just wait until after the rapture…" plan is that as we mentioned, after the rapture, God will send a strong delusion on the world. Many who have chosen to reject the offer of forgiveness of sins through Jesus, will at that time embrace the lie. It will fit right into what their hardened hearts want to hear.

As the Bible tells us, "God will send them strong delusion, that they should believe the lie, that they all may be condemned who did not believe the truth but had pleasure in unrighteousness."[33] The unwillingness of people's hearts will harden like concrete once the strong delusion comes. People will be given over to the lies they love. But why would you want to reject your loving Creator- the God who loves you so much, that He sent His only begotten (born) Son to die on the cross for your sins, and proved it by raising Him from the dead on the third day- the God who wants you to be in Heaven for eternity?

The Gospel message, the "good news" is so simple- "Christ died for our sins according to the Scriptures, He was

---

[31] Proverbs 29:1
[32] 2 Corinthians 6:2
[33] 2 Thessalonians 2:9-12

buried, and He rose again the third day."[34] It is a simple message, and the gift of eternal life is an easy thing to receive- it's a gift. It cost Jesus- the Son of God, His life- but for you, it's free! All you need to do is to turn to Him- and put your trust in Him.

You Don't Need a Preacher

You don't need a church or a preacher. You can pray- ask God to forgive your sins and ask Jesus to come into your life to be your Lord and Savior. Decide right now to put your trust in Him. It's that simple.

Another risk of the "I'll just wait until after the rapture..." plan is that you don't have any guarantees. On average, about 150,000 people die each day worldwide. Many of those people don't see it coming. Are you willing to risk your eternal destiny on the hope that you'll have more time in which to make your decision? World events are happening quickly (and life is short). If you believe what God says (and you should, since He has provided "many infallible proofs,"[35]), do it. Turn to God. Put your trust in Jesus. Don't wait. Your delay could cost you eternally.

And what if the rapture doesn't happen in our lifetime? What if the Lord holds off a little longer? If you are waiting for the rapture as proof that the Bible is true, you may breathe your last breath before the rapture happens, and your eternal destiny will be determined- you will be judged and face an eternity of separation from God and everything that is good- and end up in a place of torment.

> Sixty million people lost their lives in World War II. But the bloodshed of World War II pales in comparison to the utter devastation this world will experience in the not-too-distant future.

There is no doubt that over the centuries, there have been hundreds of millions of people who have said (regarding

---

[34] 1st Corinthians 15:3-4
[35] Acts 1:3

Jesus), "I'm just not ready right now," before slipping into their eternal destiny.

What's After the Rapture? The 7-Year Tribulation

Lastly, in regard to the "I'll just wait until after the rapture..." plan- very soon after the rapture,[36] the 7-year Tribulation period will begin. You do not want to be living on the earth at that time. It will be the worst time on earth in all of human history- by far. Regarding this time, Jesus said, "For then there will be great tribulation, such as has not been since the beginning of the world until this time, no, nor ever shall be."[37]

But if you receive Jesus before the Tribulation, and the rapture happens, you will be caught up to Heaven and will miss the entire 7-year Tribulation period. You'll be in Heaven.

Sixty-one countries and 1.7 billion people were involved in World War II. Sixty million people lost their lives. But the bloodshed of World War II pales in comparison to the utter devastation this world will experience in the near future.

About 650 years before Jesus was born, the Old Testament prophet Zephaniah prophesied about the Tribulation, quoting God, saying, "That day is a day of wrath, a day of trouble and distress, a day of devastation and desolation, a day of darkness and gloominess, a day of clouds and thick darkness, a day of trumpet and alarm against the fortified cities and against the high towers. I will bring distress upon men, and they shall walk like blind men, because they have sinned against the LORD; their blood shall be poured out like dust, and their flesh like refuse [dung]. Neither their silver nor their gold shall be able to deliver them in the day of the LORD's wrath..."[38] The Tribulation will be a time of God's judgment on those living on the earth who have

---
[36] The Bible is not specific about this- It could be a matter of days, weeks or months- according to many Bible scholars.
[37] Matthew 24:21
[38] Zephaniah 1:15-18

rejected God, and it will also be a time of severe testing for the people of the nation of Israel- "... it is the time of Jacob's [Israel's] trouble."[39]

The book of Revelation (chapters six through eighteen) lays out the events of the 7-year Tribulation- First are "the seal judgments." Beginning in Revelation chapter six, the Lord Jesus Christ begins to open a scroll that is sealed with seven seals. And with the breaking of each seal, judgment pours out: war, famine, the death of one-fourth of all people on the earth; the sun looks black and the moon looks red, meteorites fall on the earth like figs from a tree after a strong wind blows, "and every mountain and island is moved out of its place."[40] The population of the earth is panicking- "The kings of the earth, and the great men, and the rich men, and the chief captains, and the mighty men, and every slave, and every free man hide themselves in the rocks and the mountains and cry to the mountains and rocks, 'Fall on us and hide us from the face of Him who sits on the throne and from the wrath of the Lamb [Jesus]! For the great day of His wrath has come, and who is able to stand?'"[41]

Global Warming - Climate Change by Fire

The seal judgments are followed immediately by the trumpet judgments. Hail and fire mixed with blood are cast upon the earth and it results in one-third of the trees and all the grass on earth being burned up. A flaming mountain is cast into the sea, and one-third of the sea becomes like blood, killing one-third of its creatures and destroying one-third of all the ships in the oceans. A meteorite strikes the earth and affects a third of the rivers on earth, polluting the fresh water and many people die as a result. One-third of the sun, moon and stars go dark- leading to a third of the day and night being in total darkness.

---

[39] Jeremiah 30:7
[40] Revelation 6:14
[41] Revelation 6:15-17

And the next three trumpet judgments are even worse. Demons torment people, and people will try to commit suicide but will be unable to die. They'll just have to suffer through the terrible torment that comes from the demons. A great army from the east will kill one-third of the remaining population of the earth. Then will come fire, burning sulfur, lightning, an earthquake and great hail.

And the seven trumpet judgments are followed by seven bowl judgments that will be poured out at the end of the Tribulation, in which painful sores will appear on the bodies of people who took the mark of the beast. All of the oceans will be turned to blood killing every living creature in the ocean, and all fresh water will be turned to blood, and men will be scorched with fire. Then will come total darkness. The largest earthquake in human history will occur and the earth begins to fall apart- "every island fled away, and the mountains were not found."[42] One-hundred-pound hail stones fall from the sky, and this immediately precedes the return of Jesus Christ. That is the biblical description of the 7-year Tribulation on the earth.

When the rapture to Heaven happens, you do not want to be left behind. You do not want to choose "door number two" and go into the 7-year Tribulation period. But if for some reason, you end up there, all is not lost. (And maybe you are reading this book after the rapture.) You can still cry out to God for mercy. Receive Jesus as your Lord and Savior. You may have to endure some major Tribulation on the earth, and it may cost you your life (at the hands of the Antichrist and his one world governmental system), but it is far better than the alternative- eternal separation from God and Heaven- in a place of torment.[43]

---

[42] Revelation 16:20
[43] Matthew 25:46

The Tribulation Christians

The Tribulation period will be the worst time on earth in all of human history, but it will also be a time of many people entering into a personal relationship with Jesus. Speaking of the Antichrist during the Tribulation, we are told, "It was granted to him to make war with the saints and to overcome them."[44] The Antichrist will persecute "the saints"- those who have received Jesus during the Tribulation. John the Apostle tells us, "I saw under the altar the souls of those who had been slain for the word of God and for the testimony which they held."[45] Many people will put their faith in Jesus and then be killed for their faith during the Tribulation, but notice that John saw them "under the altar." People who receive Jesus during the Tribulation and who are killed by the Antichrist will be in Heaven- under the altar of God. John the Apostle says, "... I looked, and behold, a great multitude which no one could number, of all nations, tribes, peoples, and tongues, standing before the throne and before the Lamb, clothed with white robes ..."[46] and he tells us, "These are the ones who come out of the great Tribulation ..."[47] There will be a vast multitude of people who are martyred during the Tribulation. But it will all be worth it. Heaven is better than you can possibly imagine- and it will be forever.

As we will see in the next chapter, the Bible clearly predicts other major world events that will take place on earth- some possibly before or soon after the rapture, and these events will lead to a future that is far better anything we've ever known.

---

[44] Revelation 13:7
[45] Revelation 6:9
[46] Revelation 7:9
[47] Revelation 7:14

13

The End - Then the Beginning

> "For I know the thoughts that I think toward you, says the LORD, thoughts of peace and not of evil, to give you a future and a hope."
> - Jeremiah 29:11

Israel and the Antichrist

As mentioned earlier in this book, the event that marks the beginning of the Tribulation period is the confirming of a seven-year agreement that includes Israel and the Antichrist (and probably some Muslim led nations).[1] At first, many people in Israel will revere the Antichrist- "Finally, someone has brought lasting peace to the middle east!" Many will think the Antichrist is the long-awaited Messiah- the "Prince of peace." But when his "image" is set up in the temple and he demands to be worshipped as God, the Jews will realize he's not the Messiah and will reject him, he will turn on them in fury.

The prophet Zechariah seems to indicate that two-thirds of the Jewish people will be killed by the Antichrist- "And it shall come to pass in all the land,' says the LORD, 'That two-thirds in it shall be cut off and die, but one-third shall be left in it.'"[2] And apparently, many of the remaining one-third will heed Jesus' warning and flee into the wilderness,[3] where God will miraculously protect them.[4]

---

[1] Daniel 9:27
[2] Zechariah 13:8
[3] Zechariah 13:8-9; Matthew 24:16-21; Revelation 12:6
[4] Revelation 12:14

As Jeremiah predicted, "Alas! For that day is great, so that none is like it; and it is the time of Jacob's [Israel's] trouble, but he shall be saved out of it."[5] The Tribulation will be a time of severe testing for the people of Israel, but as the prophet Jeremiah predicted, "he shall be saved out of it."[6]

Many Bible scholars also believe that the place the Jews will flee to is Petra, an ancient (and currently empty) fortress city in Southwest Jordan, in the area of Bozrah. The prophet Isaiah seems to indicate that when Jesus returns to the earth, He will first go to Bozrah (Petra) to defend the Jewish people from (and destroy) the forces of the Antichrist.[7]

Beware of the Gog!

As we mentioned earlier, another last days event the Bible tells us about is what Bible students call "the Gog-Magog invasion." The prophet Ezekiel lays out what will happen in this invasion attempt but doesn't tell us exactly when the event will take place (other than the fact that it will be in the last days). It may have happened before you read this book. It could happen after the rapture. For the sake of brevity, we won't look at many details of this event, but let's consider some key events.

Ezekiel tells us that the nations- which are listed by their ancient names (many Bible scholars identify them as modern day Russia, Iran, Turkey, some central Asian Muslim nations including Kazakhstan, Uzbekistan, Tajikistan, Kyrgyzstan, Turkmenistan and maybe Afghanistan, as well as Northern Sudan and Libya), will gather together in this invasion attempt.

Ezekiel also tells us there will be infighting between these invading nations- the soldiers will end up fighting each other, and God will destroy the invading armies with a huge earthquake, massive rain, hail, burning sulfur, sickness and

---

[5] Jeremiah 30:7
[6] Jeremiah 30:7
[7] Isaiah 63:1-3

The End – Then the Beginning 153

fire. Many people around the world will realize that it must have been God that caused this massive invading force to be wiped out so dramatically. You may want to read Ezekiel chapters 38 and 39 to get the full story.

As we looked at earlier- never in recorded history has there been an alliance of these nations- until now. As of just a few years ago, Russia, Iran and Turkey are forming alliances - economic as well as military alliances. And leaders of the other nations on the list are currently led by radical Islamic regimes- and they all have one other thing in common- they all hate Israel.

Since this invasion attempt could occur very soon, what should we be expecting to see happening immediately prior to the invasion? Israel will be at peace. God says, "On that day when My people Israel dwell safely, will you not know it? Then you will come from your place out of the far north, you and many peoples with you..."[8] In the 77 years since Israel became a nation, they have never really been at peace. Radical Muslims have consistently been trying to kill Jews and wipe Israel off the map. But there is a time of peace coming- and it will precede a massive invasion attempt!

This attempted invasion may have already happened before you read this book (or it may happen soon afterwards) but it will be just one more proof that God wrote the Bible.

The Destruction of Damascus

The prophet Isaiah tells us that Damascus, the capital city of Syria, will be destroyed and will never be a city again.[9] Damascus, with a population of about two million people, is one of the oldest cities in the world. Some people who study Bible prophecy believe this event will happen when Jesus returns and judges those nations that are hostile to Israel.[10] Others believe some event may happen soon in which Syria,

---

[8] Ezekiel 38:14-15
[9] Isaiah 17:1-3
[10] Psalm 2:9

Turkey, Iran or another Islamic nation may take a weapon of mass destruction into Damascus. In order to prevent their own annihilation, Israel may decide to destroy Damascus. We don't know. The events that lead up to the destruction of Damascus are not told to us in the Bible, so we can only speculate, but at some point, the Bible tells us- Damascus will cease from being a city- it will be utterly destroyed.

The Rebuilding of the Temple

We remember that Jesus predicted that the temple in Jerusalem that existed in His day would be destroyed- "not one stone left upon another."[11] This prophecy was fulfilled in AD 70. But Jesus also predicted that during the 7-year Tribulation, the Antichrist would commit the "abomination of desolation" (that Daniel tells us will happen in the middle of the Tribulation period[12]) and immediately after the Tribulation, Jesus will return to the earth.[13]

Obviously, in order for the "abomination of desolation" to occur in the temple,[14] the temple must exist. But the temple was destroyed in AD 70 and doesn't exist as of the writing of this book. This tells us that the temple in Jerusalem will be rebuilt. The temple that existed in Jesus' day was actually the second temple. The first one had been destroyed (in 586 BC) and rebuilt years later (in 538 BC).)

We don't know the exact timing of the temple's reconstruction, but it is believed that the location of the temple was where the Muslims' Dome of the Rock now stands on the temple mount in Jerusalem.

Needless to say, this creates a serious problem. The world's Muslims will probably not appreciate the Jews wanting to rebuild their temple on a spot that modern Muslims consider to be holy. We don't know for sure, but the

---

[11] Matthew 24:2
[12] Daniel 9:27
[13] Matthew 24:15, 21, 29-30
[14] Daniel 9:27; 11:31; 12:11; Matthew 24:15-16; 2 Thessalonians 2:2:1-4

Antichrist may be the one to help facilitate the rebuilding of the temple and that may be part of the seven-year agreement with Israel. We don't know that for sure, but we do know that the temple will be rebuilt.

During the Tribulation: Witnesses, More Witnesses and a War

Two Witnesses

During the Tribulation, two "witnesses" will come on the scene and for 1,290 days (3½ years) they will prophecy and will tell people that they must turn to God. Their message will not be well received, and just as people have murdered many prophets through the years who have spoken and told people they need to turn to God (Jesus being the most well-known of them), people will want to kill these two prophets. But the Bible tells us that these two men will have miraculous power to kill anyone who tries to harm them. They will also be able to prevent rainfall and will have the power to strike the earth with plagues.[15]

But when they finish their testimony after 3½ years, the Antichrist will kill them, and their bodies will be left in the street in Jerusalem for 3½ days while the people of the earth rejoice over their deaths- even to the extent of giving one another gifts to celebrate the death of these two prophets. It seems that people worldwide will be able to see the bodies of the prophets (maybe online or on CNN, etc.). But after 3½ days, the two witnesses come back to life (causing much fear among those who see them) and will then rise up to Heaven. After their rising up to Heaven, a massive earthquake will occur, killing 7,000 people.[16]

---

[15] Revelation 11:3-6
[16] Revelation 11:7-12

144,000 More Witnesses

Also, during the Tribulation, God will raise up 144,000 Jewish men- 12,000 from each of the 12 tribes of Israel.[17] These men will be "servants" of God. It's likely they will serve God during the Tribulation by preaching the Gospel (the "good news" about salvation from judgment for sins- through faith in Jesus). These men will be "sealed" by God in order to protect them. God will mark them in order to let the angels who will be pouring out God's wrath in the Tribulation, know to not harm these men. This of course shows us that God will not pour out His wrath indiscriminately. God is all-knowing and all-powerful. He knows how many hairs are on every person's head[18] and will not "destroy the righteous with the wicked."[19]

And Another Witness- An Angel

In addition to the "two witnesses" and the 144,000 witnesses, during the Tribulation, God will also send an angel, "... having the everlasting gospel to preach to those who dwell on the earth - to every nation, tribe, tongue, and people."[20] God is "not willing that any should perish but that all should come to repentance."[21] God says, "'As I live,' says the Lord GOD, 'I have no pleasure in the death of the wicked, but that the wicked turn from his way and live."[22]

God loves people so much, that He sent His only born Son to come to the world to die on the cross to pay the penalty for our sins- to save people from the judgment for sin that we all deserve.[23] Even after thousands of years of mankind's

---

[17] Revelation 7:2-8
[18] Matthew 10:30
[19] Genesis 18:23
[20] Revelation 14:6
[21] 2 Peter 3:9- Repentance means "changing one's mind." God wants everyone to turn to Him for salvation.
[22] Ezekiel 33:11
[23] John 3:16

rebellion against God, and even during the time of God's wrath being poured out on the earth, God will still be sending the message out to humanity- "Turn to God and live- put your trust in Jesus." The fact that God will send the two witnesses, the 144,000 witnesses and the angel to preach to everyone on earth- shows that God is merciful. All people need to do is to turn to Him and to put their trust in Jesus Christ.

The Battle of Armageddon

The Battle of Armageddon will be the last world war in history and will take place at the end of the Tribulation. The Antichrist and his false prophet will lead armies from all around the world to attack Jerusalem, but ultimately, they will be fighting against God.[24] Interestingly, even now, we see a rising tide of antisemitism across the globe. The Bible describes the coming war as "the battle of that great day of God Almighty."[25] It will end with the second coming of Jesus to the earth- at which point He will slay the armies that have gathered against Him.[26]

The first time Jesus came to the earth, He came as "the Lamb of God who takes away the sin of the world."[27] Jesus is the Son of God and dwelt from all of eternity with God the Father in Heaven, and in fact, He is also God.[28] The Bible tells us that He emptied Himself of His Divine privileges and "made Himself of no reputation, taking the form of a bondservant, and coming in the likeness of men. And being found in appearance as a man, He humbled Himself and became obedient to the point of death, even the death of the cross."[29]

---

[24] Revelation 19:19
[25] Revelation 16:14
[26] Revelation 19:11-16; Isaiah 23:1-6; 63:1-5
[27] John 1:29
[28] John 1:1-3; 8:24, 58; Philippians 2:5-8; Titus 2:13; Hebrews 1:8; Isaiah 44:6 and Revelation 1:17
[29] Philippians 2:7-8

But when Jesus returns, He will not come as the Lamb. He will come as the Lion;[30] He will come in power- as the conquering King. "Now I saw heaven opened, and behold, a white horse. And He who sat on him was called Faithful and True, and in righteousness He judges and makes war. His eyes were like a flame of fire, and on His head were many crowns... He was clothed with a robe dipped in blood, and His name is called The Word of God. And the armies in heaven, clothed in fine linen, white and clean, followed Him on white horses. Now out of His mouth goes a sharp sword, that with it He should strike the nations. And He Himself will rule them with a rod of iron. He Himself treads the winepress of the fierceness and wrath of Almighty God."[31]

"Then the LORD will go forth and fight against those nations, as He fights in the day of battle. And in that day His feet will stand on the Mount of Olives, which faces Jerusalem on the east. And the Mount of Olives shall be split in two, from east to west, making a very large valley; half of the mountain shall move toward the north and half of it toward the south."[32]

Taking Care of Business

When Jesus returns to the earth at the end of the 7-year Tribulation, we (believers who are in Heaven) will follow right behind him on "white horses."[33] He will take care of business in regard to the Antichrist and his false prophet buddy- casting them into "the lake of fire" along with everyone who received the mark of the beast and respected his image.[34]

Jesus will also judge the nations. As Jesus said, "When the Son of Man comes in His glory, and all the holy angels with Him, then He will sit on the throne of His glory. All the

---

[30] Revelation 5:5
[31] Revelation 19:11-15
[32] Zechariah 14:3-4
[33] Revelation 19:11-14
[34] Revelation 19:20

nations will be gathered before Him, and He will separate them one from another, as a shepherd divides his sheep from the goats."[35]

Everyone on earth who has survived the Tribulation will be judged by Jesus. Those who are believers in Christ (and as a result- have a love for people) will enter into the "millennial Kingdom"- the 1,000-year reign of Jesus on the earth. The unbelievers- those who are indifferent to Jesus and His people, will be cast into "the everlasting fire." This may sound harsh, but people will either receive mercy (because they've trusted in the sacrifice of Jesus) or they will receive exactly what they deserve- judgment for their sins and separation from God in a place of punishment.

It is noteworthy that Jesus will say, "Depart from Me, you cursed, into the everlasting fire prepared for the devil and his angels."[36] Hell was created for the devil and his demons- not for people. But if people reject the mercy and love of God and instead choose to follow the devil's path of rebellion and hatred of God, people will end up in the same place as the devil and the demons. (And in case you are wondering- nobody will be "partying with their friends" in Hell.)

Jesus is coming back to execute God's judgment on a world population that has rejected God. The question for you is, where will you be when that happens?

Who Do You Say that I Am?

Jesus asked His followers who people said He was. People had differing ideas as to who He was. Then Jesus asked, "But who do you say that I am?"[37] That is an extremely important question. Who do you say that Jesus is? Who do you think He really is? If you think Jesus is just one of many influential figures who have lived in history- like Ghandi, Confucius, Buddha, Isaac Newton, Muhammed or Mother Teresa, you

---

[35] Matthew 25:31-32
[36] Matthew 25:41
[37] Matthew 16:15

don't know Jesus. Jesus didn't just set a great example for humanity through His self-sacrifice and love. He also made very specific claims that you either accept or reject. He said, "I am the way, the truth, and the life. No one comes to the Father except through Me."[38] In other words, Jesus claimed to be the only way to God. Jesus didn't claim to be "A way" to God. As Jesus clearly said, He is THE way to God.

There are similarities among many of the world's religions. And almost everyone would agree with some of them. For example, the idea that we should love others is a concept that is taught by numerous world religions and philosophies, but Jesus made very exclusive claims. He claimed to be the only way to God. Gautama Buddha reportedly said, "Seek truth." Jesus said, "I am the truth." Do you know the truth? Do you know Jesus personally?

Liar, Lunatic or Lord?

Jesus said, "He who is not with Me is against Me."[39] If you have not received Jesus as your Lord and Savior, you have taken a position; at this point - you are against Him. There are only three possibilities when it comes to who Jesus is. He is either a liar (and nobody should follow a liar), or He is a lunatic (a man who claimed to be God and claimed to be the Savior of the world and the only path to knowing God- many would say He must have been crazy) or Jesus is Lord- the Son of God who came to the earth He created in order to reconcile us to our Creator- who loves us. Either you accept the fact that Jesus died for your sins, and you receive Him as your Lord and Savior- or you are rejecting Him. The idea of staying neutral and thinking of Jesus as just a loving and/or a cool dude is not an option. He was either a liar, a lunatic or He is the Lord.

Have you turned to Him as Lord yet? If you haven't, do it now. The price for delaying the most important decision of

---

[38] John 14:6
[39] Matthew 12:30

your life could cost you dearly for eternity. (And having a personal relationship with Jesus is awesome!)

If you have received Jesus, live for Him. As Paul the Apostle said, "... He died for all, that those who live should live no longer for themselves, but for Him who died for them and rose again."[40]

There is no better life than a life lived for God. The things of this world are passing away. They are not worth living for. As Jesus said, "Do not lay up for yourselves treasures on earth, where moth and rust destroy and where thieves break in and steal; but lay up for yourselves treasures in heaven, where neither moth nor rust destroys and where thieves do not break in and steal. For where your treasure is, there your heart will be also."[41]

Store up treasure in Heaven by loving God, loving people and by helping others come to know Jesus. As they say, "There's only one life, it will soon be passed. Only what's done for Christ will last." Are you living for Him?

A Very Big Party in Heaven

In a traditional Jewish wedding, after a bride was "betrothed" (a legally binding engagement) to her groom, the groom would go to his father's house to prepare a place for his bride to come live with him. The Bible tells us that as followers of Jesus, He is our groom, and we ("the church"[42]) are His bride.[43] Jesus said, "In My Father's house [in Heaven] are many mansions

> The Jewish groom would arrive at the bride's house and would announce his arrival with a shout- just like Jesus' arrival to get us, His bride. We don't know exactly when, but He will arrive with a joyous shout and will take us up to Heaven- to His Father's house.

---

[40] 2 Corinthians 5:15
[41] Matthew 6:19-21
[42] Ephesians 1:22
[43] Revelation 21:9

[dwelling places]... I go to prepare a place for you. And if I go and prepare a place for you, I will come again and receive you to Myself; that where I am, there you may be also."[44]

The Jewish groom would arrive at the bride's house (the bride wouldn't know exactly when to expect him) and would announce his arrival with a shout- just like Jesus' arrival to get us- His bride. We don't know exactly when it will be, but He will arrive with a joyous shout and will take us up to Heaven- to His Father's house.

In the Old Testament, Isaac and Rebekah are a beautiful Biblical picture of Christ and His bride (the church) in the Bible. After the offering up of Abraham's son Isaac, the father sends his servant, a type of the Holy Spirit, to get a bride for his son. The servant brings the bride back to the father's house and the son leaves where his father lives to meet the bride and take her to where his father lives.[45]

Isaac came out of his father's house to meet Rebekah, his bride (who had never seen him before- like we who have not seen Jesus yet), in the field (a "spread out" place), so Jesus will come out of Heaven and descend into the clouds (in the sky- a spread out place) to meet us and He will take us back to God the Father's house. In the Jewish wedding, a wedding feast would then take place that would last seven days.[46]

As we have mentioned, just prior to the beginning of Tribulation, everyone who is trusting in Jesus at that time will be "caught up" to Heaven to be with Jesus in His Father's house. As John the Apostle tells us, "Let us be glad and rejoice and give Him glory, for the marriage of the Lamb has come, and His wife has made herself ready."[47] Many Bible scholars believe that just as a bride would spend seven days in her groom's father's house celebrating and feasting, we as the bride of Christ will spend seven years celebrating and feasting

---

[44] John 14:2-3
[45] Genesis 24
[46] www.gotquestions.org/Jewish-wedding-traditions.html
[47] Revelation 19:7

at the "marriage supper of the Lamb."[48] Needless to say, the seven years after the rapture- for those who trust in Jesus, will be a lot better than the seven years (of Tribulation) for those on earth who don't trust in Him.

Judgment for Jesus

If we are trusting in Jesus, we will stand before Jesus at the "bema" judgment. "For we shall all stand before the judgment seat of Christ."[49] Just like the competitors in the Olympics stand before the judges at the award ceremony- in order to receive their rewards, as Christians our works will be judged, and we will be rewarded accordingly. The deeds that we did- were they done in love, to please the Lord, or were they selfishly motivated? Like athletes at the Olympics, our judgement will result in rewards (no punishment)- some of us will receive greater rewards than others. The exact timing of this reward judgment isn't mentioned in the Bible, but it may be some time right after the rapture, possibly before the marriage feast.

Jews for Jesus

As mentioned earlier, during the Tribulation, many of the Jews in Israel will at first embrace the Antichrist.[50] At the midpoint of the Tribulation, when the Jews realize the truth about the Antichrist, it will be a major turning point for them. It looks like two-thirds of the Jews will be killed by the Antichrist[51] but those who aren't killed, will finally embrace Jesus as their Messiah - "And so all Israel will be saved."[52] "'And it shall come to pass in all the land,' Says the LORD, 'That two-thirds in it shall be cut off and die, But one-third shall be left in it: I will bring the one-third through the fire, will refine them as silver is refined, and test them as gold is

---

[48] Revelation 19:7-9
[49] Romans 14:10; 1 Corinthians 3:9-15; 4:1-5; 9:24-27; 2 Corinthians 5:9-10
[50] Daniel 9:27; Jesus referred to this in John 5:43
[51] Zechariah 13:8
[52] Romans 11:26

tested. They will call on My name, and I will answer them. I will say, "This is My people"; and each one will say, "The LORD is my God.""[53] Jews will be gathered from all over the earth and be taken back to Israel.[54]

satan Chained

The devil will be bound when Jesus returns and will be thrown into "the bottomless pit" for 1,000 years "so that he should deceive the nations no more till the thousand years were finished. But after these things he must be released for a little while."[55]

We won't explore this here, but there will be a 75-day period after the Lord returns (possibly including 45 days for the judging of the nations)[56] before the "millennial reign" of Jesus begins.

1,000 Years of Peace

For the next 1,000 years,[57] (the "Millennium") as the devil is chained in the bottomless pit, Jesus (along with us Christians[58]) will reign on the earth.[59] It will be a wonderful time to be alive. There will be no wars. In fact, people won't even train for war.[60] Everything on earth will be different. People will travel from all over the world to worship God in Israel.[61] People will live for hundreds of years, animals won't kill each other, and "The lion shall eat straw like an ox,"[62] so it sounds like they will be vegan. And one of the great things

---

[53] Zechariah 13:8-9. See also Zechariah 12:10-14
[54] Deuteronomy 30:1-10; Isaiah 11:11-12:6; Matthew 24:31
[55] Revelation 20:1-3
[56] Daniel 12:11-12; Matthew 25:31-46
[57] While some people believe the 1,000 years is figurative, "one thousand years" is mentioned six times in Revelation 2:2-7.
[58] Revelation 2:26-28; 3:12, 22; 1 Corinthians 6:2-3
[59] Revelation 20:4-6; See also Zechariah 14:9
[60] Isaiah 2:4
[61] Zechariah 14:16-21
[62] Isaiah 65:20-25

about the Millennium is that the devil, who is called "the tempter"[63] and "the accuser"[64] won't be around. There will be no spiritual forces (such as demons) trying to tempt people to sin.

The Final Rebellion

At the end of the Millennium, satan will be released from the bottomless pit "for a little while"[65] to tempt people and he will lead people in a final rebellion against God. Revelation tells us "Now when the thousand years have expired, Satan will be released from his prison and will go out to deceive the nations which are in the four corners of the earth ... to gather them together to battle, whose number is as the sand of the sea... And fire came down from God out of heaven and devoured them. The devil, who deceived them, was cast into the lake of fire and brimstone where the beast and the false prophet are. And they will be tormented day and night forever and ever."[66] Hallelujah.

The Great White Throne Judgment

After the devil is thrown into the lake of fire, John the Apostle tells us, "Then I saw a great white throne and Him who sat on it, from whose face the earth and the heaven fled away. And there was found no place for them. And I saw the dead, small and great, standing before God, and books were opened. And another book was opened, which is the Book of Life. And the dead were judged according to their works, by the things which were written in the books... And anyone not found written in the Book of Life was cast into the lake of fire."[67]

In the New Testament book of Hebrews, we are told, "... it is appointed for men to die once, but after this the

---

[63] Matthew 4:3
[64] Revelation 12:10
[65] Revelation 20:1-3
[66] Revelation 20:7-10
[67] Revelation 20:11-12, 15

judgment."[68] And Jesus is the One who will be the judge- "... He [God] has appointed a day on which He will judge the world in righteousness by the Man whom He has ordained. He has given assurance of this to all by raising Him from the dead."[69] The very One who died on the cross for our sins, will be the One to judge of all of humanity.

For anyone who is trusting in Jesus, you could say that our sins have all been nailed to the cross.[70] The debt, the penalty for our sins has been paid in full.[71] "There is therefore now no condemnation to those who are in Christ Jesus."[72] But for everyone who refuses to trust in the free gift of forgiveness in Christ, standing before Him at the great white throne judgment in their sins will be a terrible experience- one that will result in a terrible eternal destiny in the lake of fire.[73]

A New Heaven and Earth

Jesus said, "Heaven and earth will pass away, but My words will by no means pass away."[74] The word "heaven" carries different meanings in the Bible. It refers to the sky, to the universe, or to the place where God dwells. When Jesus said Heaven will pass away, He was referring to the sky. The God who created the universe is going to give the universe a "makeover." We will not explore that now but since it will be a major change in the universe, we mention it. God will destroy this present earth and sky with fire and will make a new one.[75] "Now I saw a new heaven and a new earth, for the first heaven and the first earth had passed away."[76]

---

[68] Hebrews 9:27
[69] Acts 17:31
[70] Colossians 2:14
[71] John 19:30; Isaiah 53:4-6
[72] Romans 8:1
[73] Hebrews 10:31; Revelation 20:15
[74] Matthew 24:35
[75] 2 Peter 3:3-12
[76] Revelation 21:1. See also: 2 Peter 3:13; Isaiah 65:17; 66:22

The Eternal State

As was mentioned in the section about Heaven, when God makes a new sky and earth, there will be a number of things that won't be around. For example- lies, sin, tears, death, mourning, crying, pain, thirst, wickedness and there won't be any lingering results from sin whatsoever- the curse of sin will be no more.[77] Everything will be perfect. And the best thing of all will be that we (who trust in Jesus) will be in God's presence forever- and in His presence "is fullness of joy."[78] That will be a fullness of joy we can only imagine at this point, but it's worth waiting for.

The New Jerusalem

A new city of Jerusalem (which is a combination of two words, which have been defined as "the Lord will provide" and "peace") will descend from Heaven (where God dwells). It will have streets and walls of pure gold, it will be radiant with crystals and precious stones, and it will be spectacular. Its splendor will be amazing beyond description. You can read a more in-depth description in Revelation chapter 21. God Himself will dwell there, and Jesus will be the light of the city. It's a place you definitely want to be part of.

There are other events that will take place in the future as well, but you now have at least an outline of what the future holds, and what the end of the world as we know it, will look like. If you have an interest in digging deeper into future world events, and are able to access them, we highly recommend the books listed in the Appendix.

You may have some questions about God and the Bible so in the next chapter, we will try to answer some questions that a lot of people ask.

---

[77] Revelation 21; 22:3
[78] Psalm 16:11

The End Times

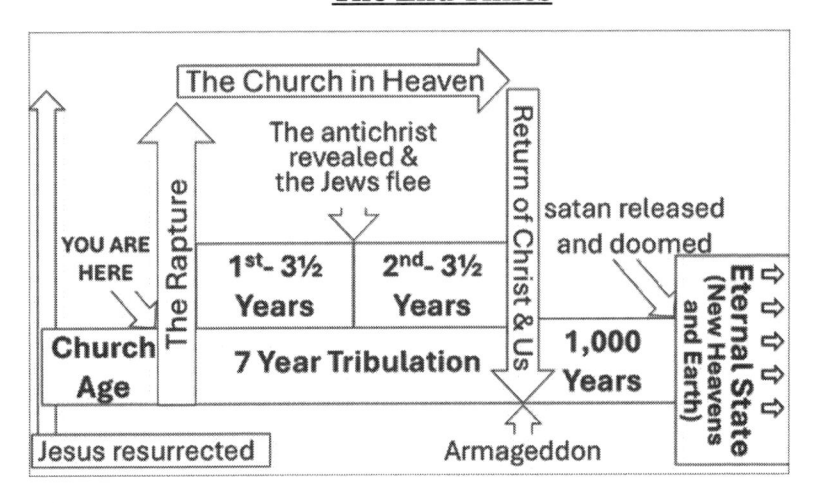

```
          The Church in Heaven →
              The antichrist
              revealed &
              the Jews flee
YOU ARE  │              │              │   satan released
HERE     │  1ˢᵗ- 3½     │  2ⁿᵈ- 3½    │   and doomed
         │  Years       │  Years       │                    Eternal State
Church   │                              │    1,000           (New Heavens
Age      │   7 Year Tribulation         │    Years           and Earth)
Jesus resurrected                  Armageddon
```

(The Rapture; Return of Christ & Us)

14

Questions People Ask

*"And you will seek Me and find Me,
when you search for Me with all your heart."*
- Jeremiah 29:13

There are some good questions people ask about God and Christianity. Knowing the answers can help people to understand what might otherwise seem confusing about God. We'll try to answer a few of these questions here-

Did Jesus really exist?

Yes, it is a well-established fact that Jesus Christ not only lived, but was publicly executed in Judea (which is now called Israel) in the 1st Century AD, under the direction of Pontius Pilate (the Roman governor of Judea), by means of crucifixion, at the request of the Jewish Sanhedrin (religious leaders). The non-Christian historical accounts of Flavius Josephus, Cornelius Tacitus, Lucian of Samosata, Maimonides and even the Jewish Sanhedrin (who rejected Jesus as the Messiah) corroborate the early Christian eyewitness accounts of important historical aspects of the life and death of Jesus Christ.

A couple of examples- the first-century Roman Tacitus (who was definitely not a Christian), who is considered one of the more accurate historians of the ancient world, mentioned Christians who suffered under Pontius Pilate during the reign of Tiberius. Suetonius, chief secretary to Emperor Hadrian, wrote that there was a man named Chrestus (or Christ) who lived during the first century.[1]

Many people watched the public crucifixion of Jesus. They saw Him get horribly beaten, tortured and then bleed to death. And they watched Him get stabbed in His side with a spear after He was dead.[2] And then (as pointed out earlier in this book), many of these witnesses were beaten, imprisoned and some were even killed rather than deny that they saw Jesus- and more importantly, that they (including 500 people at the same time) saw Him alive after He had been publicly executed. So, yes, Jesus really existed.

Has the Bible changed since it was first written?

The 39 books of the Old Testament were written from approximately 1400 BC to 400 BC. The 27 books of the New Testament were written from approximately AD 40 to AD 90. Between 3,400 and 1,900 years have passed since the books of the Bible were written. The original manuscripts have worn out and probably no longer exist. Since the books of the Bible were originally written, they have been copied again and again by scribes. Now we have copies of copies of copies of copies. So, how can we know that the manuscripts that we translate our modern Bibles from are accurate? How can we know the Bible hasn't changed over time?

Those who copied manuscripts over the years went to great measures to make sure they copied the manuscripts word for word.[3] We recommend a book by Josh McDowell, titled *Evidence that Demands a Verdict*. The book lays out a great deal of evidence. For example, there are Old Testament manuscripts of the Bible (some were written hundreds of years before Jesus was born) called the Dead Sea Scrolls, that

---

[1] Annals 15.44; www.gotquestions.org/did-Jesus-exist.html
[2] John 19:1-37
[3] For more information, see: A General Introduction to the Bible, by Geisler & Nix

were put into clay jars in the Qumran caves in Israel (around the time of Christ) and sat there for about 2,000 years.

In 1947, some shepherds found them by accident. Amazingly, the manuscripts are almost identical to the manuscripts that our modern Bibles were translated from. The few differences were "obvious slips of the pen or variations in spelling."[4]

Thousands of years of transmission (copying one manuscript to another as the older manuscripts wore out) without change? How could that be?

The Jewish people believed the Scriptures were "the Word of God" and when a manuscript was wearing out, they went to great lengths to make sure they were accurately copied. For example, when making copies of Old Testament manuscripts, they would count every letter and every word, and record in the margins such things as the middle letter and word of the manuscript. It would then be compared with the manuscript it was copied from. If a single error was found, the entire manuscript was immediately destroyed.

The "New Testament" manuscripts (written after Jesus died and rose from the dead) are also amazingly well preserved. The New Testament manuscript evidence is very impressive, with 24,000 known copies, more than 5,000 of which are complete (they include the entire New Testament). Some date as early as the second and third centuries AD.

In AD 70 (within just a few years of most of the New Testament being written), when Jerusalem was attacked by the Roman army, Jewish Christians fled to a number of other countries. They lived in these countries and now, almost 2,000 years later, manuscripts from these different countries have been found and compared to each other and they too, are almost identical.

What this tells us is that the Bible hasn't changed from when it was first written. (For more support for this claim, I highly recommend the books, *Evidence that Demands a*

---

[4] Gleason Archer, Jr., A Survey of Old Testament Introduction, 1974, Pg. 25.

Verdict, by Josh McDowell, and *A General Introduction to the Bible*, by Norman Geisler and William Nix.) Any unbiased document scholar will agree that the Bible has been amazingly well-preserved over the centuries. Even many hardened skeptics and critics of the Bible admit that the Bible has been transmitted over the centuries far more accurately than any other ancient document.

How could a loving God allow suffering?

This is one of the most common questions people ask about God. If there is a God, and if God is a God of love, then why would God allow suffering?

God is love.[5] And because God is love, He created humanity in a way that would allow each one of us to know His love and to love Him in return, as well as to love others. Love requires freedom of choice. If we were all created like robots- programmed to behave in certain ways, we couldn't love.

Let's say that we were to create a robot that was programmed to respond in a certain way to certain stimuli, and it automatically said to you, "I-love-you," there would be something missing. It wouldn't be the same as if a human being was to sincerely choose to say, "I love you," because they really love you. Love requires the ability to choose.

Because God is love, He created us with the freedom to make choices- the ability and freedom to love and to hate. As a result of people having the ability to make choices, we can choose to love or reject God. We can choose to love sin and hate God. When people choose to be prideful, greedy and selfish, there will be many other choices they make that will result in suffering for others and for themselves. The root cause of all suffering is sin. And the results of sin are devastating. But because God is love, He has decided to allow us to have freedom of choice, even though (for a time) there will be a lot of suffering as a result of humanity's choosing to

---

[5] 1 John 4:8

love sin. And of course, not all of our suffering is a result of our own sin.

If a person decides to light their neighbor's house on fire, it can result in terrible consequences for their neighbor, for themselves, and for others as well. Sin can have a ripple effect that goes far beyond the person who commits the sin. But God has allowed us to have the ability to choose because He knows the value of love.

Love is so wonderful, that God is willing to allow sin and suffering for a time. From our perspectives, it may seem like the suffering on this earth has been going on forever. But as God tells us, "For what is your life? It is even a vapor that appears for a little time and then vanishes away."[6] As we looked at in this book, for those who choose to love God and to receive His mercy, the time of suffering will soon come to an end- forever. We will all be in Heaven where there will be absolutely no suffering- ever again.

God is willing to allow humanity's suffering for a season, in order to eternally bless those who choose to turn to Him to receive His love and mercy.

God also uses suffering. If a child carelessly runs on a road and trips and hurts himself, he can learn from that suffering. People often learn very valuable lessons through suffering. The saying, "No pain, no gain," is not absolutely true, but pain and suffering can be good teachers. Suffering can also help to humble us- to set us free from the terrible sin of pride.

In the lives of Christians, God uses suffering to help make us more like Jesus. Sometimes we suffer for doing what God wants us to do,[7] and we know that suffering is a part of life.[8] God uses suffering in our lives to help us to mature in our

---

[6] James 4:14
[7] Matthew 5:11-12; John 15:18-19; 1 Peter 4:12-13
[8] John 16:33

faith,[9] to help us have compassion on others,[10] and it can also be God's loving discipline in our lives[11]- to help us to learn.

What about people who have never heard of Jesus?

How can a loving and fair God condemn anyone and not let them into Heaven, when they have never even heard of Jesus? The Bible tells us that "The heavens declare the glory of God; and the firmament (the sky) shows His handiwork. Day unto day utters speech, and night unto night reveals knowledge. There is no speech nor language where their voice is not heard. Their line has gone out through all the earth, and their words to the end of the world."[12] It also says, "since the creation of the world His invisible attributes are clearly seen, being understood by the things that are made, even His eternal power and Godhead, so that they are without excuse."[13]

God reveals certain things about Himself through creation. How can someone look at a beautiful sunset, a starry sky, a beautiful forest or a lake, (or the cuteness of a baby or a puppy or kitten) and honestly think it all happened by random chance? We can't. The Bible also tells us that God has given every one of us a conscience.[14] Cultures all around the world believe that murder is wrong. Is that because they all communicated with each other and entered into a mutual agreement? No, it's because God has put it in every person's conscience- murder is wrong. On the day of judgment, every person will be judged according to their conscience. And as we have seen in this book, we are all guilty of violating our consciences.

So, is everyone who hasn't heard of Jesus, going to Hell? God is all-powerful. He will not force Himself on you or on

---

[9] James 1:2-4. See also: www.gotquestions.org/why-do-Christians-suffer.html
[10] 2 Corinthians 1:3-4
[11] Hebrews 12:5-11
[12] Psalm 19:1-4
[13] Romans 1:20
[14] Romans 2:14-16

anyone, but He can and does intervene in people's lives and miraculously reveal Himself to them. As I share about in my life story,[15] I had absolutely no interest in Jesus, but He used a series of miraculous events to get my attention. He appeared to Moses[16] and the Apostle Paul miraculously[17] as well as to others in the Bible. And God can reveal Himself to anyone He wants to reveal Himself to, in any way He wants to. In fact, millions of Muslims in the middle east have put their faith in Jesus as a result of dreams and visions in which they say Jesus has revealed Himself to them.

You might say, "Well then, why doesn't God reveal Himself to me right now?" I believe God is revealing Himself to you right now, through this book. You might say, "No, I want to see God. Why won't He show Himself to me or perform a miracle to prove to me that He is real?" God is gentle. He will not force Himself upon you, but God promises that if you whole heartedly seek Him, you will find Him.[18] God will be found by anyone who honestly seeks Him.

And the reality is, nobody comes to faith in Christ through a miracle. It might be part of the process, but the Bible says, "faith comes by hearing, and hearing by the word of God."[19] Even though God did miracles to get my attention, it wasn't until I heard the message of the Gospel (the good news) on the radio, that I received Jesus as my Lord and Savior. You don't need miracles in order to believe; you simply need to receive the message from God- the Gospel. God loves you. Jesus died for your sins and rose again on the third day. If you haven't received Jesus as your Lord and Savior, I suggest that before you become too concerned about any Pygmies in Africa who haven't heard of Jesus, that you make sure you have reserved your place in Heaven. And a great way to "hear" the

---

[15] A Different Life- The Strat Goodhue Story (available for free upon request)
[16] Exodus 3:1-4
[17] Acts 9:1-6
[18] Jeremiah 29:13-14
[19] Romans 10:17

word of God is through reading the Bible. You might want to get a Bible and pray to God to speak to you through it as you read it- and see what happens.

Is the God of the Bible sexist?

Why does the Bible call God, "He" and "Him"? "God is Spirit."[20] Since God is Spirit, God is not what we would commonly think of as "male" or "female." In fact, the Bible tells us, "God is not a man..." (a human being).[21] God is not a sexual being, nor is "He" a biological male. In the Book of Genesis, we are told, "God created man in His own image; in the image of God He created him; male and female He created them."[22]

We see from this verse that all people are created in the image of God- and we are created male and female. So, both men and women are created in the image of God. Men are not in any way superior to women. Nowhere does the Bible say or imply that men are better, smarter or more spiritual than women. Women and men are both created in the image of God.

There are a number of verses in the Bible where the more feminine characteristics of God are revealed. "As the eyes of a maid to the hand of her mistress, so our eyes look to the LORD our God."[23] And God says, "Now I will cry like a woman in labor..."[24] and "How often I wanted to gather your children together, as a hen gathers her chicks under her wings."[25]

In fact, Jesus was considered a revolutionary in the way He treated women. Women were considered by many in the culture of Jesus' day, to be second class citizens, but Jesus stood up for women and gave them honor. In fact, after rising

---

[20] John 4:24
[21] Numbers 23:19
[22] Genesis 1:27
[23] Psalm 123:2
[24] Isaiah 42:14
[25] Matthew 27:37

from the dead, the first person Jesus appeared to was a woman.[26]

So, why does the Bible refer to God as "He" and "Father" etc.? God contains all the qualities of both male and female genders, but He has chosen to present Himself with an emphasis on masculine qualities of fatherhood, protection, strength, etc. Metaphors used to describe Him in the Bible include: King, Father, Judge, Husband, Master, and the God and Father of our Lord Jesus Christ.

Since that is how God refers to Himself, that should be good enough for us. And God loves and values women just as much as He loves and values men.

Do Christians hate homosexuals?

No. God loves people, but He hates sin. Christians should also love people, including homosexuals (and LGBTQ+); and should hate sin. The Bible clearly teaches that just as pride, selfishness, greed, strong sexual desires (other than for one's own spouse), gossip, slander, stealing and other things are sins; so is homosexuality.[27] God desires that every one us would live according to how He designed us to live. God created people a certain way but because of mankind's sinful nature, we may have desires that are not pleasing to God and are not good for us.

It is often the case that we don't choose our attractions. Someone may feel like they have an orientation toward lying, anger, lust, stealing, gossip or homosexuality, but that doesn't mean those behaviors are therefore ok with God, or good for us. But God understands and cares. And God is able to help us to resist temptation, no matter how strong the temptation is. In fact, resisting the temptation to sin may be the most difficult struggle we will face in our lives,[28] but God wants to

---

[26] Mark 16:9
[27] Genesis 1:26-27; Leviticus 18:22-30; Jude 7; Romans 1:26-27,32; 1 Timothy 1:9-10; 1 Corinthians 6:9-11
[28] Hebrews 12:4 (NASB)

help us (through the power of His Holy Spirit) to live in ways that are pleasing to Him and good for us. That's one of the things about receiving Jesus as your Lord and Savior- the power of God's Holy Spirit comes into your life, and you are able to resist temptation.[29]

Back to the point of Christians hating homosexuals; it is a very sad thing that some ill-informed and immature Christians, as well as many so-called "Christians" do hold hatred in their hearts toward homosexuals. Those people are not following Christ in that attitude. Jesus died to pay the penalty for every sin- including homosexuality. And Jesus commanded us to love our neighbors as ourselves.[30]

Every one of us is a sinner. We all fall short. Every Christian should love homosexuals, and as far as I'm aware of, all the Christians I know- do love homosexuals (and LGBTQ+ people). If you are LGBTQ+ and you go into a Christian church where you don't feel loved- find another church.

What's the next step as a new follower of Jesus?

Becoming a follower of Jesus is as easy as **A-B-C:**

- **A-** Admit you are a sinner- "for all have sinned and fall short of the glory of God."[31] Repent- turn to God.
- **B-** Believe "that Christ died for our sins according to the Scriptures, and that He was buried, and that He rose again the third day."[32]
- **C-** Confess Jesus as Lord- "if you confess with your mouth the Lord Jesus and believe in your heart that God has raised Him from the dead, you will be saved."[33]

---

[29] 1 Corinthians 10:13
[30] Mark 12:31
[31] Romans 3:23
[32] 1 Corinthians 15:1-4
[33] Romans 10:9

You may find it helpful to (sincerely) pray a prayer to God such as, "Dear God, Please forgive me for my sins. Jesus, Thank you for suffering and dying on the cross for my sins and for rising again from the dead on the third day. Please come into my life and be my Lord and Savior. Help me to follow You. In Jesus' Name I pray, Amen."

If you are trusting in Jesus as your Lord and Savior, you are "born again."[34] The Bible tells us that when God poured out His Holy Spirit when the church first started, "... they continued steadfastly in <u>the apostles' doctrine [teaching]</u> and <u>fellowship</u>, in <u>the breaking of bread</u>, and in <u>prayers</u>."[35] God desires for us to get to know Him and to please Him.

First, He wants us to "continue steadfastly in the apostles' doctrine (teaching)"- Get a Bible (the New King James Version is a great translation) and read it regularly. It is very helpful to (prayerfully) read the Bible every day. (A suggestion is to read the Book of John, then read through the entire New Testament and then read the Old Testament.) Jesus compared "the word of God" to eating. He tells us, "Man does not live by bread alone, but by every word that comes from the mouth of God."[36] We should read the Bible regularly (preferably daily) in order to be strengthened in our faith.[37] (It can also be very helpful to memorize Bible verses that really stand out to you- think and pray about them.)

Secondly, and tied into the point of learning from God's Word (the Bible), those who believe in Jesus should "fellowship." That means gathering regularly with other believers in Jesus. An essential part of us growing in our relationship with God (and in pleasing God) is to gather with other Christians.[38] It will be very helpful if you can find a church or fellowship to be part of that believes the Bible is

---

[34] John 3:3-7
[35] Acts 2:42
[36] Matthew 4:4
[37] Psalm 1; 119:9; Romans 10:17
[38] Hebrews 10:24-25

"infallible and inerrant"- that the Bible is completely trustworthy and has no errors. While there are slight variations in translations, it is clearly proven by the 100% accuracy of the hundreds of fulfilled prophecies in the Bible, that even though the manuscripts were written by men, they were truly "God-breathed."[39] God superintended the writing of the Bible. (You shouldn't be part of a church that doesn't really believe the Bible.) Many would also recommend trying to find a church that teaches through the Bible (verse-by-verse teaching) as opposed to one that just teaches "from" the Bible.

Thirdly, the "breaking of bread"- or "communion" as it is commonly called. By regularly commemorating the death of Jesus, it helps us to remember (and proclaim) what He has done for us until He returns. For more information, you might want to check out: www.gotquestions.org/Bible-communion.html.

Fourthly, prayer is vital to our relationship with God. Just as a child talking and listening to their parents is important, so is our communication with God. It's great to follow the example of King David who said, "My voice You shall hear in the morning, O LORD; in the morning I will direct it to You, and I will look up."[40] You can pour out your heart to God in prayer (and pray for others). He is your loving Father and He hears your prayers (even if they aren't out loud).

Jesus also directed His followers, saying, "When you pray, say: Our Father in heaven, Hallowed be Your name. Your kingdom come. Your will be done on earth as it is in heaven. Give us day by day our daily bread. And forgive us our sins, for we also forgive everyone who is indebted to us. And do not lead us into temptation, but deliver us from the evil one."[41] Needless to say, this is a great prayer to pray.

---

[39] 2 Timothy 3:16
[40] Psalm 5;3
[41] Luke 11:2-4

Lastly, as an act of obedience to God, it is important to get baptized (immersed in water "in the name of Jesus"). Jesus said, "He who believes and is baptized will be saved; but he who does not believe will be condemned."[42] We can see from that statement, that you don't need to be baptized in order to be saved from the judgment of sin, but baptism is something that God commands us to do.[43]

The act of baptism is an outward expression of the inward reality of change that happens in the life of every person who puts their trust in Jesus. It demonstrates that the old way of life has ended, and a new life of faith in Jesus Christ has begun,[44] and baptism symbolically identifies the new believer with the death, burial, and resurrection of Jesus Christ. You might want to look for a good Bible believing church where you can be baptized. For more information, check out: allaboutgod.com/water-baptism.htm

If you have questions about God or want to grow in your relationship with God, you might want to check out gotquestions.org and/or www.allaboutGod.com. Blueletterbible.org is also a great free online resource for Bible study. And it would be very helpful for you to go to a Bible-believing, Bible-teaching church. People say a lot of things about Christians and about God. Instead of forming your opinions from second and third hand accounts, why not find out for yourself? Jesus loves you.

---

[42] Mark 16:16
[43] Acts 2:38
[44] 2 Corinthians 5:17

If you were blessed by this book, or if you received Jesus as your Lord and Savior after reading it, we'd love to hear it. You can email us at: **timeisshortfreebook@gmail.com**

(And please consider leaving a positive review on amazon.com)

Appendix 1: Ten Proofs for the Pre-tribulational Rapture

"I will come again and receive you to Myself; that where I am, there you may be also."
- John 14:3

Can we know the timing of the rapture?

While the timing of the rapture in relation to the Tribulation is not an essential teaching of the Christian faith, we believe it is an important one. What we believe affects how we live. We as Christians should be "eagerly waiting" for the Second Coming of Christ.[1] If we are expecting (3½ or) seven years of God's wrath to be poured out all around us before the rapture happens, how can we be "eagerly waiting"?

And in light of the amazing rate at which end times prophecies are being fulfilled, it seems we may very well be on the verge of the beginning of the Tribulation. If that is the case, then people who believe Christians will need to endure 3 ½ or seven years of God's wrath on the earth before we get raptured should be storing up beans, blankets and bullion to get them through the Tribulation.

Here are 10 reasons why our "blessed hope"[2] is truly blessed- why we don't need to store up beans, blankets and bullion for the Tribulation. We shouldn't be looking for years of God's wrath being poured out on people all around us. We should be "eagerly waiting" for the Lord to come in the clouds

---

[1] Hebrews 9:28; Romans 8:23, 25; Philippians 3;20; 1 Corinthians 1:7
[2] Titus 2:13

at any moment to take us to Heaven. The rapture is "imminent"- it truly could happen at any moment! Here are some of the reasons why we can know we will be "caught up" before the Tribulation-

1) As mentioned in Chapter 10, Jesus said in John 14:2-3, He will come and take us to where He is, in His Father's house in Heaven.[3] The entire focus of this passage is on us being with Jesus in Heaven. Proponents of a "post-Tribulation rapture" (rapture after the 7-year Tribulation) believe that at the 2nd coming of Jesus, He will come part way from Heaven, stop in the clouds and rapture us, and then immediately bring us back down to the earth again, where we will reign with Him for 1,000 years.

But Jesus said, "I will come again and receive you to Myself; that where I am, there you may be also." He's coming from Heaven to receive us, so that where He is (in Heaven) we will be also. This doesn't line up with the post-tribulation position that Jesus is preparing a place in Heaven for us "that where I am, there you may be also," but He won't take us there- at least not for 1,000 more years.[4]

Some post-tribulation rapture believers say the focus of this passage is simply on "being with Jesus" but in reading the passage, that really doesn't seem to be the main focus. Rather, the focus is being with Jesus in the Father's house- that's in Heaven, not on the earth. Here's a rewording of John 14:2-3 that expands on what Jesus is saying by inserting the locations He is talking about. Let's see if the post-tribulation rapture view makes sense- "In My Father's house [in Heaven] are many mansions [in Heaven]; if it were not so, I would have told you. I go [to Heaven] to prepare a place for you [in Heaven]. And if I go [to Heaven] and prepare a place for you [in Heaven], I will come again and receive you to Myself; that where I am [on earth?], there [on earth?] you may be also."

---

[3] John 14:2-3; 1 Thessalonians 1:9-10; Mark 16:19; Luke 24:51; 1 Peter 3:22
[4] After the 1,000 year- Millennial reign of Christ on the earth.

That doesn't make sense. Jesus went to Heaven,[5] is in Heaven,[6] is preparing a place for us in Heaven, will come from Heaven[7] and will take us to Heaven.

2) As mentioned in Chapter 10, in writing about the Tribulation, Paul the Apostle writes, "... God did not appoint us to wrath, but to obtain salvation..."[8] The mid-tribulation and post-tribulation rapture proponents claim that God will protect Christians on earth during the Tribulation. But almost the entire 7-year Tribulation is described as the time of God's "wrath."[9] How could God protect the Christians in Hawai'i, for example, during the Tribulation, when "... every island fled away, and the mountains were not found."?[10] How could even one single Christian in Hawai'i survive when every island and mountain is gone? One-hundred-pound hailstones will be falling from the sky, "and hail and fire followed, mingled with blood, and they were thrown to the earth. And a third of the trees were burned up, and all green grass was burned up,"[11] and at least one-half of the world's population (possibly 5 billion people) will die during the Tribulation. In fact, God tells us that the Tribulation will be so severe, that if He didn't stop it, nobody on earth would survive. [12]

The Bible tells us of three purposes of God bringing the Tribulation to the earth- "Behold, the day of the LORD comes, cruel, with both wrath and fierce anger, to lay the land desolate; and He will destroy its sinners from it... I will punish the world for its evil, and the wicked for their iniquity; I will halt the arrogance of the proud, and will lay low the

---

[5] Mark 16:19
[6] 1 Thessalonians 1:10
[7] 1 Thessalonians 4:16
[8] 1 Thessalonians 5:9
[9] Revelation 6:16-17; 11:18; 14:19; 15:1, 7; 16:1
[10] Revelation 16:20
[11] Revelation 8:7
[12] Matthew 24:22

haughtiness of the terrible."[13] First, God will destroy the wicked; second, He will break people's pride- so that many non-Christians will turn to God and ask for His mercy, put their trust in Jesus and be forgiven of their sins.

The third purpose of the Tribulation is to "test" and "refine" the people of Israel.[14] It is "... the time of Jacob's trouble, but he shall be saved out of it."[15] (God changed Jacob's name to Israel.[16]) Since these are the purposes of the Tribulation, there is no reason for us as the church to go through the Tribulation. There will be Christians on earth (referred to as "saints"[17] and "the elect"[18]) during the Tribulation (these are people who come to faith in Christ during the Tribulation- many of whom will be killed by the Antichrist[19]). But the Bible never mentions the church as being on earth during that time.[20]

It is not consistent with the character of God to pour out wrath on those who are trusting in Him. We are told that when God was going to judge Sodom and Gomorrah, Abraham was concerned about his nephew Lot who was living in Sodom. Abraham prayed to God, "Would You also destroy the righteous with the wicked? ... far be it from You! Shall not the Judge of all the earth do right?"[21] God physically removed Lot from Sodom before He judged Sodom, and He will

---

[13] Isaiah 13:9, 11
[14] Zechariah 13:8-9
[15] Jeremiah 30:7
[16] Genesis 32:38
[17] For example- Revelation 5:8; 8:3, 4; 11:18; 13:7, 10; 14:12; 15:3; 16:6; 17:6; 18:24; 19:8; 20:9
[18] For example- Matthew 24:24, 31; Mark 13:22, 27. Note: The church (on earth from the day of Pentecost until the rapture) are all saints and elect of God, but not all the elect and saints are part of the church. Just like (until recently) all Boy Scouts were boys, but not all boys were Boy Scouts.
[19] Daniel 7:21-22; Revelation 7:9, 14; 13:7; 14:12-13
[20] It's noteworthy that "the church" is not mentioned after Revelation Ch. 3- because we are in Heaven until we return with Christ in Revelation Ch. 19.
[21] Genesis 18:23, 35

physically remove Christians from the earth before He judges the earth. As people say, "I don't believe Jesus is going to beat up His bride before the wedding."

3) In speaking about the Tribulation, Jesus said, "But take heed to yourselves, lest your hearts be weighed down with carousing, drunkenness, and cares of this life, and that Day come on you unexpectedly. For it will come <u>as a snare on all those who dwell on the face of the whole earth</u>. Watch therefore, and pray always that you may be counted worthy to escape all these things that will come to pass, and to stand before the Son of Man."[22] Jesus is clearly talking about the Tribulation, and what does He say? "Pray ... that you may be counted worthy to <u>escape all these things</u> ... <u>and to stand before the Son of Man</u>." We don't want to be among "all those who dwell on the face of the whole earth" when the Tribulation comes suddenly, like a trap. We want to "<u>escape all these things</u>" and be standing before Him instead. It seems that Jesus is speaking of a pre-tribulational rapture.

4) According to the mid-tribulation and post-tribulation rapture views, God will protect the church on earth during the Tribulation. In the letters to the seven churches in the book of Revelation- "He who has an ear, let him hear what the Spirit says to the churches,"[23] Jesus says to the Philadelphian church, the church that correlates to the current church age (time period)- "Because you have kept My command to persevere, I also will keep you from <u>the hour of trial which shall come upon the whole world</u>, to test those who dwell on the earth."[24] "The hour of trial which shall come upon the whole world, to test those who dwell on the earth," is clearly referring to the Tribulation. And this is a clear promise to keep the church out of the entire time-period of the Tribulation.

---

[22] Luke 21:34–36
[23] Revelation 2:7, 11, 17, 29; 3:3, 13, 22
[24] Revelation 3:10

This is very different than saying the Lord will keep the church "through" the Tribulation. He says He'll keep us "from"- (Greek- ek)- "out of, away from" the "hour of trial." In other words, He will keep us "out of, away from- the time period of the Tribulation." That seems to clearly speak of a pre-tribulation rapture. The church will not be on earth during any of the time of the Tribulation. We are to "... wait for His Son from heaven ... even Jesus who delivers us FROM the wrath to come,"[25] not "Jesus who delivers us IN or THROUGH the wrath to come."

5) As pointed out in Chapter 10, Jesus specifically mentioned both Noah and Lot being physically separated before God's wrath was poured out.[26] He could easily have just mentioned life going along as usual and then judgment coming, if that's all that Jesus intended to point out. He could have mentioned Noah's and Lot's days but not included "until the day that Noah entered the ark"[27] and "but on the day that Lot went out of Sodom..."[28] But in both cases, Jesus points out the specific order of events- the physical separation takes place before the wrath of God was poured out. We will be raptured, and then the wrath of God will be poured out on the earth.

6) It seems noteworthy that in looking at "types of Christ" in the Bible- Moses, a type of Christ in the Bible, was rejected by his brothers (like Jesus was) and received his bride (like Jesus will) before he passed through the tribulation under Pharoah.[29] Joseph, also a type of Christ- received his bride, during the time of his "rejection by his brethren," and before the 7-year famine, which could be seen as a type of the 7-year Tribulation. And the 7-year famine was a time of trials for his

---

[25] 1 Thessalonians 1:10
[26] Admittedly, a number of Bible scholars do not interpret these passages as referring to the rapture.
[27] Luke 17:27
[28] Luke 17:29
[29] Exodus 2:21-25

brethren, like the Tribulation will be "the time of Jacob's [Israel's] trouble."[30]

The rapture is similar to what happened to Enoch before the flood. The Scriptures tell us that "Enoch walked with God; and he was not, for God took him."[31] At the rapture, God is going to take His people (those who "walk" with Him) to Heaven just as He took Enoch.

And as we looked at in Chapter 10, Isaac and Rebekah paint the most beautiful picture in all the Bible of Jesus and His bride, the church. The Son comes out of the Father's house to receive His Bride and take her back to His Father's house. Isaac didn't meet Rebekah part way and then immediately take her back to where she had been living. He came out from his father's house and took her back to his father's house. And Jesus will come out of His Father's house (Heaven) and take us back to His Father's house (Heaven) as well. This is perfectly consistent with the sequence of events in ancient Jewish weddings- the groom would come and surprise his bride and take her back to his father's house, where he had prepared a place for her to live.

7) In the book of 1 Thessalonians, the rapture is explained and then the Tribulation is mentioned. We see the order of rapture - then wrath.[32]

8) In 2 Thessalonians, chapter 2, Paul the Apostle tells us about the timing of the rapture. Three and a half years into the Tribulation, when the Antichrist goes into the temple, he will want to be worshipped as God. As Paul tells us, "Let no one deceive you by any means; for that Day will not come unless the falling away comes first, and the man of sin is revealed, the son of perdition, who opposes and exalts himself above all that is called God or that is worshiped, so that he sits

---

[30] Jeremiah 30:7
[31] Genesis 5:24
[32] 1 Thessalonians 4-5

as God in the temple of God, showing himself that he is God."[33]

The Greek word translated as "falling away" is "apostasia." The Greek noun apostasia is only used twice in the New Testament- combining of apo - "away from" and istemi - "to stand."[34] So, it has the core meaning of "to stand away from" or "departure." Jerome's Latin Bible translation known as the Vulgate, from around AD 400 renders apostasia as the word "discessio," meaning "departure." The first seven English translations of the Bible all translated that word in 2 Thessalonians 2:3 as "departure" or "departing."[35] The first Bible translation that departed from this interpretation was the Douay-Reims [Roman Catholic] translation in 1582. That's about 1200 years of Bible translations that rendered apostasia as "departure."

The Liddell and Scott Greek Lexicon defines "apostasia" as either "a defection or revolt" or a "departure or disappearance."[36] The word could mean either "to stand" physically or spiritually "away from." The verb form of this word is used fifteen times in the New Testament. (Vines Expository Dictionary defines the word as "depart".) Again, the "departure" could be spiritual or physical. Examples of physical departures- After an angel led Peter out of a Roman prison, the angel "departed"[37] from Peter. Paul also prayed

---

[33] 2 Thessalonians 2:3-4
[34] The Rapture in 2 Thessalonians 2:3, Thomas D. Ice, Liberty University, tdice@liberty.edu
May 2009
[35] (1384) Wycliffe Bible, (1388) Wycliffe-Purvey, (1526) Tyndale Bible, (1535) Coverdale Bible, (1539) Cranmer Bible,
(1540) Great Bible, (1576) Breeches Bible, (1583) Beza Bible, (1608) Geneva Bible
[36] Henry George Liddell and Henry Scott, A Greek-English Lexicon, Revised with a Supplement [1968] by Sir
Henry Stuart Jones and Roderick McKenzie (Oxford, Eng.: Oxford University Press, 1940), p. 218
[37] Acts 12:10. See also: Luke 4:13

that his physical affliction would "depart" from him.[38] The verb is also used in the exhortation to "withdraw" from ungodly men.[39]

Many Bible scholars believe this passage in 2 Thessalonians chapter 2, lays out the biblical timeline. "That Day"- is referring to the Day of the Lord (spoken about in the Bible, which includes the 7-year Tribulation period). So, the rapture (the physical departure of all the Christians on earth) happens first, and then the Antichrist goes into the temple and wants to be worshipped as God. As Paul writes"... that Day [which includes the 7-year Tribulation] will not come unless <u>the falling away [the departure- the rapture] comes first</u>, and the man of sin is revealed."

Secondly, regarding Paul's mention of "the departure"- A departure from the faith would be a very difficult event in history for Christians to clearly identify. There have been many defections from the faith- starting at the time of Adam and Eve and continuing all the way through Paul's day. So why would Paul mention a spiritual departure from the faith as a sign to look for? On the other hand, the rapture- a physical departure from the earth- would be a very clear and easy event to identify. So, it makes sense that Paul is speaking of the rapture, rather than a (difficult to identify) spiritual departure from the faith.

Paul then repeats and expands on that same sequence of events in the very next verses, saying, "Do you not remember that when I was still with you I told you these things? And now you know what is restraining, that he may be revealed in his own time. For the mystery of lawlessness is already at work; only He who now restrains will do so until He is taken out of the way. And then the lawless one will be revealed, whom the Lord will consume with the breath of His mouth and destroy with the brightness of His coming."[40]

---

[38] 2 Corinthians 12:8
[39] 1 Timothy 6:5
[40] 2 Thessalonians 2:5-8

The Holy Spirit working in the church (i.e.- "He who restrains" and "what is restraining"), will be "taken out of the way,"- raptured to Heaven, and then the Antichrist, "the lawless one" will be revealed. We see that Paul repeats the same sequence of events that he laid out in the preceding verses- Rapture first, then Tribulation.

9) The post-tribulation rapture view can't explain where "sheep" come from at the end of the Tribulation: Speaking of His return to the earth, Jesus said, "When the Son of Man comes in His glory, and all the holy angels with Him, then He will sit on the throne of His glory. All the nations will be gathered before Him, and He will separate them one from another, as a shepherd divides his sheep from the goats."[41]

Here is the problem: If the rapture is post-tribulational and not pre-tribulational, then when the Lord comes back to the earth, there not going to be any sheep (believers) among "the nations" to separate from the goats (unbelievers). That separation would have just taken place at the rapture.

The rapture is the "catching up" of all believers ("the sheep") to meet the Lord in the air. Once that occurs, <u>only</u> non-believers (the "goats") will be left on the earth. Therefore, no separation would be necessary. Who, then, who are the sheep who are separated from the goats?

The answer? After the <u>pre-tribulational</u> rapture (during the 7-year Tribulation), many people on earth will receive Jesus. These are the "sheep" who will be separated from the "goats" for judgment at Jesus' Second Coming to the earth.

10) During the Tribulation, some people will know when Jesus will return to the earth:

The Bible tells the exact timing of the return of Christ to the earth. The prophet Daniel wrote about the beginning of the Tribulation, when the Antichrist will make (or enforce) an agreement with Israel, "Then he shall confirm a covenant with many for one week [literally- one "seven"]; But in the

---

[41] Matthew 25:31–32

middle of the week ["the seven"] he shall bring an end to sacrifice and offering. And on the wing of abominations shall be one who makes desolate..."[42] As we looked at earlier, the Antichrist will make a 7-year agreement with Israel and at the mid-point- 3½ years into the agreement, he and his forces will commit "the abomination of desolation" in the temple and "they shall take away the daily sacrifices, and place there the abomination of desolation."[43] That is "the image of the beast"[44] that the false prophet sets up in the temple.

Jesus links the "abomination of desolation" with the Tribulation[45] and tells us, "For then there will be great tribulation, such as has not been since the beginning of the world until this time, no, nor ever shall be."[46] And then Jesus tells us when He will return- "<u>Immediately after the tribulation</u> of those days the sun will be darkened, and the moon will not give its light; the stars will fall from heaven, and the powers of the heavens will be shaken. Then the sign of the Son of Man will appear in heaven, and then all the tribes of the earth will mourn, <u>and they will see the Son of Man coming</u> on the clouds of heaven with power and great glory."[47]

So, Jesus will return to the earth "immediately after the Tribulation." That means when people on earth see (online and on CNN, etc.) the image of the beast set up in the temple, they can mark their calendars. It will be exactly 3½ years (1,290 days) until Jesus returns to the earth.

But Jesus speaks to His followers, saying, "Watch therefore, for <u>you do not know what hour your Lord is coming</u>... Therefore you also be ready, for the Son of Man is coming at an hour you do not expect."[48] How do we reconcile

---

[42] Daniel 9:27
[43] Daniel 11:31
[44] Revelation 13:14-15
[45] Matthew 24:15-21
[46] Matthew 24:21
[47] Matthew 24:29-30
[48] Matthew 24:42, 44

Jesus' statement that He is coming at a time when Christians on the earth won't expect Him to come, with the Bible's detailing of exactly when Jesus will return to the earth? It's easy- the first aspect of Jesus' coming will be "at an hour you [His followers] don't expect"- that will be the rapture, and the second aspect of His coming (His return to the earth) will be "immediately after the Tribulation."[49]

The rapture is the first of two aspects of Christ's return to the earth. The idea of two aspects of the coming of Christ is nothing new. There were actually two aspects of the first coming of Jesus as well. He was born in Bethlehem- with the pronouncement of the angels, the shepherds, and all of the things that happened on the day of His birth.[50] Then, thirty years later, He came as King to Jerusalem as foretold by the prophets Daniel and Zechariah.[51] This was the second aspect of His first coming.

Since there were two aspects of Jesus' first coming, we should not be surprised that there will be two aspects of His Second Coming. The first part being the rapture, the second part being the coming of Jesus to the earth to set up the Kingdom.

For more information, we recommend reading the book, *The Rapture Question*, by John Walvoord.

---

[49] Matthew 24:29-31
[50] Matthew 2:1; Luke 2:1-20
[51] Daniel 9:24-25; Zechariah 9:9; Matthew 21:1-11

Appendix 2: Questions About the Rapture

Is the Rapture a "new" teaching?

Many people falsely believe that the rapture is a recent invention, and that the idea of the rapture was first thought of in 1830 by a man named John Darby.

We believe it's clear from the Bible that the Old Testament, Jesus and the Apostles taught the pre-tribulation rapture. Highly respected "early church fathers"- pastors who led the church in the early centuries of the Christian church's existence, also believed in the rapture of the church- and even a "pre-tribulation" rapture.

Records show that quite a few Early Church Fathers- Irenaeus, Polycarp, Papias of Hierapolis, Clement of Rome, Barnabas, Tertullian, Cyprian, Chrysostom all believed in a pre-tribulation rapture. The Shepherd of Hermas in the year AD 150 preached a pre-tribulation rapture and Victorinus proclaimed it in the year AD 270.

For example, Irenaeus (a student of Polycarp, who was a student of John the Apostle) wrote: "And therefore, when in the end the Church shall be suddenly caught up from this, it is said, 'There shall be tribulation such as has not been since the beginning, neither shall be.' For this is the last contest of the righteous, in which, when they overcome they are crowned with incorruption."[1] Irenaeus used the Greek word "harpazo" ("caught up")- the same word Paul the Apostle used in 1 Thessalonians 4:17 to describe the rapture.

Eusebius, an influential defender of the Christian faith (born around 265, died around 340) wrote, "Indeed, as all

---

[1] Against Heresies, 5:29. Note: While some quote Irenaeus as teaching a post-tribulational rapture- it seems that is due to their misunderstanding of his use of the word "church."

perished then except those gathered with Noah in the ark, so also at His coming ... the cataclysm of the destruction of the ungodly shall not happen before those men who are found of God at that time are gathered into the ark and saved according to the pattern of Noah ... all the righteous and godly are to be separated from the ungodly and gathered in the heavenly ark of God. For IN THIS WAY [comes the time] when not even one righteous man will be found anymore among mankind."[2]

And Ephraim the Syrian in AD 350 wrote, "All the saints and elect of God are gathered together before the tribulation, which is to come, and are taken to the Lord, in order that they may not see at any time the confusion which overwhelms the world because of our sins."[3] The pre-tribulation rapture is clearly not a modern invention.

Regarding the rapture, the Bible tells us, "And the dead in Christ will rise first. Then we who are alive and remain shall be caught up together with them in the clouds to meet the Lord in the air. And thus we shall always be with the Lord. Therefore comfort one another with these words."[4] For every person who puts their faith in Jesus as Lord and Savior, the coming rapture is a tremendous source of comfort. We will be caught up to be with the Lord in Heaven. We will be rescued before that "dreadful" day that takes place on the earth. And we will be in that place that is so wonderful, that, "Eye has not seen, nor ear heard, nor have entered into the heart of man the things which God has prepared for those who love Him."[5]

If you haven't yet received Jesus as your Lord and Savior, do it right now. "Behold, now is the day of salvation."[6] If you

---

[2] Recent Pre-Trib Findings in the Early Church Fathers, by Lee W. Brainard, Pg. 46
[3] Pseudo-Ephraem (c. 374-627). Source: The Rapture in Pseudo-Ephraem by Thomas Ice
[4] 1 Thessalonians 4:16-18
[5] 1 Corinthians 2:9
[6] 2 Corinthians 6:2

have received Him, live for Him[7] and pray and share Christ with others while there is still time. As Jesus said, "Go into all the world and preach the gospel to every creature."[8] He loves you, and Time is Short!

Are all Christians going to be raptured?

The short answer is: Yes. All true Christians who die before the rapture or who are alive on the earth at the time of the rapture will be "caught up" to be with the Lord in Heaven. Maybe when you are reading this, the rapture has already happened and from what is being reported, not all Christians have disappeared. The reason for this is that not everyone who says they are a Christian, is really a Christian.

The Bible warns about the dangers of believing in "another Jesus" and "a different gospel," [9] and says, "But even if we, or an angel from heaven, preach any other gospel to you than what we have preached to you, let him be accursed."[10]

In fact, when the disciples asked Jesus about His return and "the end of the age," the first thing Jesus did was to warn them, "Take heed that no one deceives you."[11] He warned, "Then many false prophets will rise up and deceive many."[12] There are millions of Jehovah's Witnesses and Mormons (members of "The Church of Jesus Christ of Latter Day Saints") who claim to be Christians but they preach and believe in a different Gospel and have a very different Jesus than the one revealed in the Bible. This will be clearly shown after the rapture when almost all of them, and many Roman Catholics (and others who believe their good works will get them to Heaven) along with many other so-called Christians

---

[7] 2 Corinthians 5:15
[8] Mark 16:15
[9] 2 Corinthians 11:4
[10] Galatians 1:8
[11] Matthew 24:4
[12] Matthew 24:11

who haven't received Jesus as their Lord and Savior- will be left on the earth.

There are many false religions and false prophets and teachers that we don't have the space in this book to list, but you can know that if the rapture has happened, and there are a bunch of "Christians" who are still on the earth; they weren't really Christians. Going into a church doesn't make you a Christian any more than going into a donut shop makes you a donut, or going into a lake makes you a fish.

But the Bible also tells us that after the rapture, many people will become followers of Jesus and will end up in Heaven. There will be "a great multitude which no one could number, of all nations, tribes, peoples, and tongues, standing before the throne and before the Lamb, clothed with white robes, with palm branches in their hands, and crying out with a loud voice, saying, 'Salvation belongs to our God who sits on the throne, and to the Lamb!'"[13] All that Mormons, Jehovah's Witnesses and other so-called Christians need to do to have their sins forgiven is to turn to the true Jesus Christ and the true Gospel- as revealed in the Bible.

For more information about Mormonism ("The Church of Jesus Christ of Latter-Day Saints")- check out mrm.org. For more info regarding Jehovah's Witnesses (devotees of the Watchtower Society)- check out jwfacts.com.

For general questions about God, Jesus and the Bible, check out: www.gotquestions.org. For a great free online Bible study resource, check out: www.blueletterbible.org.

---

[13] Revelation 17:9-10

Appendix 3: Recommended Books for Further Study

For Information on Prophecy and the End Times:

The End Times in Chronological Order, by Ron Rhodes

Charting the End Times, by Tim Lahaye & Thomas Ice

The End, by Mark Hitchcock

What Lies Ahead, by J.B. Hixson and Mark Fontecchio

The Spirit of the Antichrist- Volumes I and II,
Spirit of the False Prophet, &
The Great Last Days Apostasy: How the American Church Is Falling Away, by J.B. Hixson

The Encyclopedia of Biblical Prophecy, by J. Barton Payne

The Rapture Question, by John Walvoord

For Information About the Bible:

Evidence that Demands a Verdict, by Josh McDowell

A General Introduction to the Bible, by Geisler and Nix

A Survey of Old Testament Introduction, by Gleason Archer, Jr.

Bible Study on the Web: www.blueletterbible.org

Other Books by Strat Goodhue-

How to Know the Will of God- Living a Life of Knowing God's Will, Right Decision Making, and Intimacy with God

A Different Life- The Strat Goodhue Story
(Free copy available upon request)

The Place of Joy-
Finding Joy and Meaning in Life in the 21st Century

Strat's books can be found on: **www.timeisshort.net**

To Order Free Copies of This Book-

To order free copies of this book to give away, email us at: **timeisshortfreebook@gmail.com**

If you would like to make a tax-deductible donation to support the effort to print and distribute this book, email us for our mailing address, scan this QR code or go to:

www.venmo.com/u/Time_is_Short

<u>**100%** of donations will be used for printing and shipping costs.</u>

> "For God so loved the world that He gave His only begotten Son, that whoever believes in Him should not perish but have everlasting life. For God did not send His Son into the world to condemn the world, but that the world through Him might be saved."
> - John 3:16-17

Jesus loves you!